DONIE
O'SULLIVAN
A FOOTBALLER, ONCE

WITH JIMMY O'SULLIVAN DARCY

HEROBOOKS

PUBLISHED BY HERO BOOKS
1 WOODVILLE GREEN
LUCAN
CO. DUBLIN
IRELAND

Hero Books is an imprint of Umbrella Publishing
First Published 2022
Copyright © Donie O'Sullivan and Jimmy O'Sullivan Darcy 2022

ISBN 9781910827222

Cover design and formatting: jessica@viitaladesign.com
Photographs: The O'Sullivan family collection

DEDICATION

As son m'anamchara 's mo chéile, Áine, a d'imigh romhainn le
deanaí agus ar son mo thuismitheoirí

Who gave so much and asked for so little

Gan dearmad ar an t-aos óg: Saoirse, Caoilinn, Siúin, Oran,
Lochlann, Cuán, Ruairí, Cian, Síofra,
Ferdia, Ailbhe agus Croíadh

« PROLOGUE »

IF YOU GO down to Kerry over the next while, ask the people you meet down there if they know Donie O'Sullivan? You'll be surprised at the answer.

It will always be, 'Which Donie O'Sullivan?'

Donie is a popular name in Kerry nowadays, and always was as far back as I can remember. As for O'Sullivan? Lord love you, if you tried to call a meeting between all the Donies and all the O'Sullivans from Kerry... well, it would take a while as they gathered themselves.

That's if they bothered to come at all – you may as well know now that Kerry breeds stubbornness in both men and cattle.

'Which Donie O'Sullivan?'

There's the CNN reporter. We value the Cahirsiveen man, he really does us proud.

There's a Donie O'Sullivan working out in Liebherr, and probably more than one – Liebherr are big employers around here. There's one that worked as a kitchen porter, or maybe it was in the bar actually, in one of the local hotels. Actually, it must have been the bar. *How would I have met him in the kitchen?*

I certainly know of one who is a builder, and another a chemist. There's at least two farming – one of them has a son of the same name in college. Neither of these is Donie 'Farmer' O'Sullivan. That Donie was a substitute on the Spa team that won their historic East Kerry breakthrough final in 1966, while his more famous namesake led the team from centre-back to the club's first, and arguably most famous, victory. Donie 'The Farmer's' brothers, Andy and John were chairmen of Spa (Andy) and London (John) simultaneously. None of them, of course, were farmers, but they came from farming stock.

No, you are looking for Donie O'Sullivan... *the footballer.*

THAT WOULD BE Donie O'Sullivan of Spa.

Donie would be *the footballer.* He'd be many other things, too... teacher, raconteur, philosopher, very much philanthropist and, most importantly, father... but he'd be Donie 'The Footballer' for very good reason. Everybody plays football in Kerry, but there aren't too many of them who have nine East Kerry Championships (note – be careful how you talk about the East Kerry Championship around here).

The trophy is officially known as the O'Donoghue Cup, but a lot of people here call it the 'Dr Paddy'... a kindly soul who helped many a family who couldn't always afford the luxury of a doctor's fee.

Four county championships are his too. That's the Bishop Moynihan Cup... and Bishops were a strong power in this land. Donie, a man whose religion is quiet-spoken but deep down at his core, grew up playing football.

Donie would win those county championships with East Kerry, an amalgamation of clubs who don't qualify for the senior club championship. These days, Kerry have eight clubs and nine divisional teams in the senior county championship. The big advantage is that a player from a small club can star on the big days and play his way onto the Kerry team. Traditionally, most counties draw their players from the big clubs.

Donie has a Kerry intermediate medal as well, and there is a story behind that one. Donie was proud to play with Dr Crokes at the start of his playing career and has always held that great club, unquestionably the kingpins of Killarney down through the years, in great affection and esteem. Spa, hit in the early-60s by emigration like so many other rural areas then and now, was defunct at the time. Donie O'Sullivan already had two O'Donoghue Cups in East Kerry by the time attempts were made to revive the club in the better economy of the 60s.

He was not just an established county player; he was well established as one of the best footballers of a generation. Dr Crokes hadn't broken the hegemony of the mighty John Mitchels of Tralee, with the sons of John Joe Sheehy on board, who won five county championships on the trot. But a full-strength Dr Crokes were bound to break through that barrier sooner or later. There was no sensible reason for a footballer of Donie's stature and ability, a Gaelic Sports All Star in 1965-66, to join a newly reformed Spa.

Except that Donie was an adopted son, a beloved one, of Dr Crokes. He was a native of Spa from the cradle.

It was and remains his place and his people. When Spa came calling, Donie answered. And let the record show that Jackie Looney, one of the great Crokes players, and a teammate and friend, who was secretary of the club in the mid-60s, informed Donie on the steps of the Franciscan Church in Killarney that he had already signed the transfer form.

Spa reached the East Kerry final at their first attempt in 1966. They won, and went on to add six more before Donie finished. Mind you, Jackie had 10 by the time he finished, and when Colm Cooper and Eoin Brosnan broke that record, Jackie Looney had been one of their first trainers. Medals are only bits of metal; Jackie, and Donie, for that matter, have left and still leave deeper legacies.

Spa won the Kerry intermediate and, towards the end of Donie's playing career, they pipped a star-studded Austin Stacks to the county league title – the Stacks team that included the O'Keeffes, Ger Power, Tim Sheehan, Denny Long, and many more. Spa had some great players of their own who all stood together.

YES, IF YOU ask for the Donie O'Sullivan who played football, you will find the right man. But Donie doesn't and hasn't ever identified himself as a footballer.

In Spa, he has always been a neighbour, and a very popular one. In St Brendan's College, where he was never identified as a footballer at all, and Maynooth and UCD, where he most certainly was, he was a scholar, and one who has always loved knowledge for its own sake.

In Tralee, he was always a teacher. A stern enough one, if truth be told. Donie always sought to challenge his students to draw the best out of themselves. He was always as proud of the mediocre student, who had to struggle to pass exams, as the gifted ones who got the highest marks. He maintained a high standard but did a lot more carrying than pushing. Teaching is a real art in itself, and requires as much an understanding of psychology (one of Donie's areas of expertise) as the subject itself.

In the summers, he spent a lot of time in California, at the University of San Diego, where he was known as an expert lecturer on Irish-American studies from his time at the Glucksman Institute in New York University.

Donie studied psychology in New York after leaving Maynooth. He was playing for the college team, St John's, and a couple of the New York Jets footballers watched him as they were entering and leaving the famous Shea Stadium in Queens. Donie is justly famous for having a prodigious kick, and the Jets were looking for a place-kicker (if you don't know the rules of American Football, I honestly recommend checking them out. It is a far more subtle and complex game than one might think from first impressions).

The Jets arranged trials and liked what they saw; a professional contract was put forward. Donie gave it real consideration, but life was already pulling him in a different direction. Some American Football fans out there might still remember the quietly talented Irishman who smiled as he was photographed with the legendary quarterback Joe Namath.

Donie calls that decision in his life as an 'epiphany', with someone, somewhere directing him to make the right choice in life.

Among the players that he met on the field, not just his teammates but also the opposition, he always was and still is known as a great friend. While you are talking to Donie – and he will talk to you, he is a very easy-going man and comfortable with a vast array of subjects – the discourse will be almost inevitably be interrupted by a phone call from a friend. Some of those friends are among the most famous GAA players of all time; some will be famous in other fields on both sides of the Atlantic Ocean. Some won't be famous at all, which makes absolutely no difference whatsoever.

DONIE O'SULLIVAN HAS far more friends than football medals and knows which, by far, has the greater value.

More than anything else, Donie is a family man. A lot of the things that Donie is most celebrated for are very much of his own making. He worked for his football and his education and his living, and his character was moulded both internally and by the background of his family and his community. But the best thing that ever happened to Donie was to meet his future wife, who was at least his equal, a girl named Áine.

Áine and Donie married in June of 1971. They had more than 50 years together, and a family comprising Colm, Fionnuala, Eoin and Orna. Dr Áine O'Sullivan (née King) passed from this life, and Donie's life, in 2021.

Yes, Donie O'Sullivan the footballer is a man worth talking to, and if you ever get the chance, you should do it. But you should have the clear understanding that you are talking to far more than a footballer.

*The Kerry team (Donie is second from right in the front row)
before the 1965 All-Ireland final in Croke Park.*

« CHAPTER 1 »

THERE IS NO point in trying to understand or appreciate anyone who grew up in Donie O'Sullivan's era without understanding the social and cultural background. When he was a boy, Ireland as a republic was not much older.

Ireland in the 1940s was closer to what life had been like for their great-grandparents than it would be for their children. Ireland had partly freed itself from the tenacious grip of the British Empire and become a nation in its own right. It had taken a lot of bloodshed, and there was no shortage of heroes – or villains – on all sides, but the guns were finally falling silent across the Irish countryside. It was an uneasy peace, but peace nonetheless.

Éamonn De Valera, whose American birth had probably saved him from the firing squad after the Easter Rising, would lead the Government of Ireland from 1932-48 and indelibly put his personal stamp on the character of a young and relatively uncertain nation. He would also serve two more terms as Taoiseach and as President.

He was inarguably a visionary and a dedicated patriot. He didn't just dream of a free gaelic Ireland; he worked tirelessly to make it happen. He got many, many things right and he gave unstintingly of himself to help the Irish people.

Instead of judging, De Valera, Donie prefers to quote from Bryan McMahon's autobiography, 'The Master'… *I consider the greatest mistake any commentator can make is to pass judgement of 'then' in the context of 'now'. To do this is to ignore the prevailing atmosphere of a particular era and hold it up to unjust scrutiny or ridicule by applying to it standards that now prevail in a completely altered set of circumstances.*

De Valera outlined his ideal of Irish society in a famous St Patrick's Day radio broadcast in 1943. 'The ideal Ireland that we would have, the Ireland that we dreamed of, would be the home of a people who valued material wealth only as a basis for right living, of a people who, satisfied with frugal comfort, devoted their leisure to the things of the spirit.'

It wasn't so much that most Irish people in the 1940s were 'satisfied with frugal comfort' – it was that they didn't exactly have too many other options. In fact, it's fair to say that frugal comfort was at least as much an aspiration as a reality for a huge amount of Irish people.

Just one in four houses had running water when Donie was born. The ESB had commenced in 1927 but, by '46, only a third of Irish homes, almost all urban, had access to electricity. The Rural Electrification Scheme started that year. The best that rural dwellings could hope for in Donie's childhood would be to have one of the relatively new Tilley lamps that gave much better light than before. Electricity finally came to Tiernaboul in August 1955.

Ireland's economy was almost entirely dependent on agriculture and the British market (the setting up of the Ford factory in Cork in 1930 was a notable exception). The Great Famine, and the awful laissez-faire policy of the British Government at the time that made it so much worse than it should have been, still very much cast a shadow over people.

To us now, the famine is a terrible footnote of the mid 19th century, but in the 1940s it still lived in oral memory, especially with so many people dependent on the harvest. Tourism and services were under-developed, while industrial manufacturing was virtually stagnant.

'All over Europe in the late 1920s and 30s there was a conservative reaction to the weakening of traditional values that had happened during The Great War,' observes Donie. 'It is not surprising that life in the Irish Free State took on a conservative Catholic ethos.

'The government was as anxious as the clergy to preserve what was regarded as traditional values.

'Once colonised, a people often depend substantially on their religious practices, over which they have still some control and which recall a time when they had the dignity of freedom.'

Irish Catholicism was an enormous source of solace to people – for many, their local priest was their advisor, friend, and intermediary with authority.

It was the church who provided most education. It may have curtailed artistic development – and writers like Brendan Behan, Seán Ó Faoláin, Austin Clarke, Samuel Beckett, JP Donleavy and Aldous Huxley. But it is very worth remembering that while the church may have been responsible for people's choice in reading, it was also the reason why so many of them *had* the ability.

TO KEEP ITS struggling economy afloat, Ireland relied very heavily on the export of cattle to Britain... and its young people all over the world. In the past, 85 percent of Irish emigrants left for the United States, which witnessed the largest population influx in world history in the latter half of the 19th century. The economic collapse caused by the Wall Street crash in 1929 meant that during the 1930s the bulk of them were going to Britain. But they were going – 100,000 of them in the 1930s, jumping to 250,000 a decade later and over 400,000 in the 50s.

A fledgling Ireland dreamed of self-sufficiency, and its government tried to implement that. A proud young nation was busily rejecting the forcibly imposed British culture, looking inward to Ireland's ancient language, culture, and customs. The spirit of national pride was understandable but insular – and it came with a cost at a time when the Irish economy was dependent and controlled by Britain.

Then, the ideologies of nations and the fading of empires sparked a conflagration that would engulf the whole world. At least 70 million people died in the Second World War. Ireland remained steadfastly neutral, albeit clearly sympathetic to the allied cause. This, then, was the somewhat bleak Ireland that Donie O'Sullivan was born into. He and his generation experienced an economic, educational and social revolution that was far less bloody, but far more impactful than any that had happened before.

Are you reading this by an electric light?

Do you have access to post primary education?

Do you have a heating system in your home?

A fridge?

Then you should be thanking his generation.

They grew up with none of those things, and they are the reason why you did.

DON'T BOTHER LOOKING for Spa on the map – Spa doesn't exist as a geographical certainty, more as a conglomeration of townlands bonded by a common identity.

The name originally comes from a well in Tullig that supposedly (and quite probably did – old country remedies were usually derived from good reasons, i.e. everyone knew that dock-leaves were a good antidote to a nettle sting long before they knew the difference between alkaline and acidic) had healing properties. In a 19th century that saw the doctrines of Newton and Descartes take precedence over the bible, and economies prosper over traditional landholders and gentry, travelling to spas had become hugely popular for the middle and upper classes (including royalty) in England.

Royalty have visited Killarney many times, both from England and other countries. Queen Victoria, better known in this country as the 'Famine Queen', paid the most famous visit to Killarney in 1861. She neglected to visit Spa along the way, and maybe no harm either.

There was no real political agitation and only a subdued sort of embryonic nationalism among the very few people around Spa, who had both the education and the leisure to even think such thoughts. Making a living was hard enough; such visits were important to the gentry and part of a world that was alien to small farmers and cottiers who eked a living here.

In Ireland, memory is often short, selective and slanted to suit the political and commercial interests of the day, noted Dr Tom Horgan in 'The Stones Still Speak'. *On a superficial level the history of Killarney would appear to have begun in 1861 with the visit of Queen Victoria, whose three-day presence brought regal approval to the tourist industry. But the mountainsides that the queen surveyed had been denuded by their populations by starvation, disease and evictions little more than a decade earlier. Land ownership was by right of conquest and the common people toiled as serfs on the lands of their ancestors.*

There sometimes seems to be a timelessness about history. Here is how the Irish poor and middle class lived, almost unchanging for centuries until the Industrial Revolution, and even that didn't make huge changes in rural Ireland where hard labour was the dominant factor. Where living is hard, so is providing a living for children, and there are migratory patterns all over rural Ireland of the late 19th century. Emigration is obviously the most profound one, but even that is almost never the simple heartbreaking story of song and story. Donie's own family are a case in point.

'My grandfather, Tim was actually born in the US, his own father had emigrated… he was referred to as Timmy the Yank. He came back to Ireland when he was about 16,' explains Donie.

'Not everybody who left made fortunes. In fact, most didn't, and that's as true now as then. He came back with enough money to buy a small bit of land and a cottage west of Killorglin, and that is where my father, Michael grew up. It was a strong republican area, and my father certainly believed in the republican system of government.

'Four or five of his family had already left for the United States… my grandfather having been born there made it easier and there were not any options at home.

'You had a better chance out there at that time; there was little in Ireland, especially if you ended up on the wrong side after the Civil War. When there was *little* in the United States, and a recession hit there, some people came home. That's how life worked itself out; it wasn't always planned or anything like that.

'My father left in either 1923 or '24, emigrating to Boston. He was the second youngest, and the only one to ever come back and live in Ireland.

'My mother was Catherine Murphy, and she came from Annaghmore, a couple of miles up here near Raheen Cross. Her father had spent years in Buffalo. He had been taking Dan Murphy, the grandfather of Bishop of Kerry Bill Murphy to Headford Station by horse and cart.

'He had attended the "American wake" for Dan – emigration was "cosúil le mbás"… like a death in the family.

'The pair set out around dawn, with my grandfather thinking about things along the way. He must have been doing a lot of thinking… he left the horse and cart at the station for collection and joined Dan on the journey.

'He spent years there before coming back to raise a family.

'My mother left in 1925, when she was just 17 years old, and her sister left two years later when she was the same age… just 17, heading off from Queenstown. It must have been a scary thing for them both.

'My mother and my father met over there.

'A lot of her family had already walked the same path. I know she had two sisters, my aunts, who lived the United States; one of them, Mary, lived to be 100 years old.

'I know I have many first cousins in America, but I don't know who they are and I've never met them.

'Emigration was rife back then; my family's story is similar to many others from the time. My parents met in Boston, and my brother, Tim was born there.

'The likelihood is that they would never have come back only for the Great Depression… things were as bad in the US then as they were in Ireland. My father was a talented musician. He worked as a labourer on the building sites over there, but he loved playing music.

'Things were booming in the States in the 20s, and then… everything collapsed. My parents were able to scrape together enough to purchase a dwelling house, as I mentioned earlier… and a few acres of stony soil.

'My father never really talked to us about that period in his life. He would get five dollars playing his music. He didn't drink, and money was scarce. One night he was coming home with his few dollars. It was late at night and many degrees below freezing, and he could see three or four people under a bridge… sleeping rough.

'They knew my father and they approached him, looking for some spare change, if he had any and… didn't my father know them too.

'One of them was his own first cousin.'

TO SUGGEST TO a young Donie O'Sullivan that he had a very hard life would have puzzled the youngster. His family, like the vast majority of their neighbours, were small farmers up in Tiernaboul.

All the place-names around an area that was always understood to be 'Spa' have maintained their Irish titles. Minish (Maigh Inis – the 'plain by the island'), Clasheen (cloisín – a clos is a 'hollow' and 'ín' is a diminutive attached to anything, i.e. 'the small hollow'), Lissivigeen (Lios Uí Bhuigín – Biggin or Beggan's fort), Ardanaenig (Ard an Aonaigh – quite literally 'the height of the fair', an Aonach was a cattle mart and an occasion of festivity), Coolcaslach (the 'back of the lake'), Knockmanagh (cnoc meanach, the middle hill)… and several more.

Tir na bPoll itself is the 'Land of Holes', which will tell any half-decent farmer plenty about the quality of the farmland. And a lot more about the lack of quality

– it was hard, stony ground, and eking a living was not easy.

Donie's family, then, were not living in luxury. But very few people were, and the idea that Donie grew up hungry or deprived of basics would be nonsensical. Donie's parents were raising their children in better circumstances than they themselves had been raised, and their own parents would have been raised up close enough to the shadow of the Great Famine.

The famine was a real memory in people's lives. The Workhouse was now St Columbanus Hospital, but many older people had a real dread of the place.

No, what we would call poverty was actually a reasonably decent standard of living, and Donie was among a generation of children who were close enough to hard memories of yore to appreciate the difference.

DONIE HAD A good upbringing within a widely respected and liked family and a very strong community. It's something of a cliché now to say that everybody knew each other back then, but it's also a simple truth.

The idea of a solitary farming family......it's as oxymoronic as saying a 'hermitic socialite' or a 'deafening silence' or, as the famous joke would have it according to soldiers everywhere... 'military intelligence'.

The weather has regulated human life ever since the first monkey climbed down from the trees, started finding out that these opposable thumbs could be useful, and discovered that walking upright gave a better view of approaching dangers. Farming was beginning to change fast when Donie was a child, with machinery becoming more commonplace, but the vagaries of the Irish weather could still make or break small farmers.

Children had to do their chores.

There were six children in the O'Sullivan household, Tim being the eldest. 'We were quite close growing up,' says Donie. 'We played football together. He went to St Kieran's in Kilkenny to study and was ordained in 1961. He is still going strong as a priest, though he's semi-retired now and living in Derby. He worked most of his life in the Nottingham diocese.'

Tim was three years older than Donie, and then there was Maureen, Joan, John and Marian. All the siblings were working as much as playing while growing up. That goes for the girls as well as the boys, by the way. Feminism was a virtually unheard of concept in those uncomplicated times. Women weren't equal under the law by any means, but they were usually equal under their own roofs and when work was to be done, everybody was expected to get it done. And they did.

Cows were moved to the different few pastures in their turn and fed hay in the winter (silage was not in common use at all in those days, and reduced the terror of unexpected rainfall considerably for farmers who depended on hay). Turnips got thinned (sliced into pieces) and animals were fed.

Pigs were very valuable animals and there's truth in the old saying that the only part that isn't used is the squeal. Eggs were gathered – and if eggs weren't being found… well, plucking a chicken is easier than you think. Curiously enough, fish was a rare enough supplement to the Irish diet, except during Lent and Fridays. Fields were ploughed and planted and harvested. Turf was cut and dried – the best turf had the colour, and was close to the consistency, of coal. The hay was cut and stacked and gathered in its time. Picking stones out of fields for ploughing was an annual and difficult, monotonous chore. Buried stones tend to work their way to the surface, and potatoes don't grow on stones.

You know those picturesque ditches in fields of walls made of stones that look so beautiful in Ireland? The craftsmanship of their construction was and is a valued art, but the material always lay close to hand. Especially in Tiernaboul, where you would sometimes find as much stone as soil. Cooking, cleaning, and clothing were full-time occupations.

Sometimes, nowadays, you will hear people lament for the days when life was simple and idyllic. Easy to tell that they never lived it; life was certainly not simple and even less idyllic in those times than now, but life was then and still is now a wonderful adventure.

Co-operation was not so much a philosophy as an essential way of life. The meitheal, the gathering of neighbours to get work done, was vital at both ploughing and harvest. What one family knew would very soon be communal knowledge. People also had a far broader understanding of politics at local, national, and even global levels than is commonly supposed.

Small farmers, remember, depend on the price of cattle and crops for their living, and those prices sway with prevailing circumstances. Marx had very little to teach such people. The old saying, 'Ar scath a cheile a mhaireann na daoine' (the people live in one another's shadow') was no metaphor. It was a literal truth. Their prosperity was your prosperity and the vice in the versa of that was also a literal truth.

With masterful irony, the greatest conflagration and conflict the world has ever known, far greater than the 'war to end all wars' of a generation before, was known as 'The Emergency' in Ireland.

To a very young Donie, the most that meant was the occasional sighting of a strange airplane in the sky, a brief source of wonder and delight for a child.

THE WORK DIDN'T mean that there wasn't time for play; of course, there was. There were army forts that needed building, gunslingers to be the faced down on imaginary main streets at high noon, the occasional red Indian raid that needed fending off. Don't bother with any well-meant guff about Native Americans.

Most of these children had aunties and uncles in America who were native Americans in their eyes and would send parcels (a white suit for First Communion was a sign that the parcel had arrived) and sometimes money home. Often, money enough for a ticket for the next sibling or relative to take that long journey to a new and more prosperous, but often lonelier, life.

Not that there has ever been any point in moralising to children – cops and robbers were arbitrary decisions and you could switch sides as often as you wanted. Mischief was limited in an area where every neighbour's child was known for miles around in a tight community, but the occasional bit of mischief was indulged in anyway.

Discipline was strict by modern standards, but not cruel – I wouldn't be so sure that the pendulum hasn't gone a little bit too far the other way now.

One thing that you wouldn't see much of is diversity. Everyone was Caucasian and almost everyone was Catholic. There is no right or wrong in that; it's just a statement of fact. Diet was healthy but predictable. Don't mind curries or pizza or the like. Rice was consumed as rice pudding with a dollop of jam and spaghetti was… look, oranges and tomatoes were rare enough to be considered exotic.

In 1957, the BBC famously put out a broadcast on April Fool's Day about Italy's spaghetti crop in danger of failing… most of England believed it (so much so that they had to retract it rapidly).

The only reason it didn't worry too many people around Spa, or Kerry in general, is because they had about as much access to spaghetti as they did the BBC. Sweets were a treat.

Bulls Eyes, black jacks, sherbet, liquorice, toffees, pear and apple drops, barley sugars, jellies, chocolate of course… children weren't spoiled, but they weren't spoiled for occasional treats either.

Buttermilk was a popular treat in itself.

The children didn't wear shoes from March to October, and didn't want to anyway. In fact, most harness-makers doubled up as cobblers. Timmy McCarthy had a shoe shop in Killarney town, as did the Hilliards, who were a very prominent family. The children in Tiernaboul would all know Mrs. McCarthy, who taught in the school, but they would have little reason to visit her husband's business. New shoes would be rarer than new clothes, and if you had older siblings, new clothes would be plenty rare enough.

Sure, with the strong tradition of naming children after grandparents (first son was paternal grandfather, first girl was maternal grandmother, etc.), even names were recycled. In many cases, you even inherited your political allegiances. In Spa, you were republican, but not necessarily staunch. People worried more about feeding their families than freeing Ireland, but it was there in the background.

The War of Independence and the Civil War were very recent events for a society that had long memories. And Tiernaboul had as much reason as anywhere else in the country to remember.

LET'S TAKE A journey with Donie along these narrow roads and hedges. There are passing landmarks that an uncaring stranger might pass by unheeding, but to Donie these are what the poet called *the dolmens of my childhood*.

If you are coming into Killarney along the Cork Road, you'll pass Glenflesk. Paddy Healy was one of the great early Kerry footballers – he more than anyone started football in that area and he won All-Irelands in 1909 and '10. It was called Headford then; the modern incarnation of St Agatha's GAA Club was formally founded in 1951, but there were always footballers in the area.

Past that, as you draw closer to Killarney, is Minish. That's the beginning of Spa. Just after the railway crossing, down on the left there is the house that the Olympian Gillian O'Sullivan came from. Further on is John A. Woods, a huge business. Across the road from that is Mick Gleeson's, arguably the best footballer to come out of this area – all of the Gleesons, boys and girls, were footballers and good ones.

Lissivigeen school is at the Gillian O'Sullivan roundabout. Mike McAuliffe was a very good footballer; his father Joe coached hundreds of kids from Spa. They didn't all become great athletes or great players, but all of them were the better as people because of Joe. To your right is Lissivigeen and Ardanaenig.

Football already existed in the area; Spa would enter a team in the 1942 Kilcummin Parish League and beat Clashnagarrane in the final. Spa footballers like the Flemings, Caseys, and Morris brothers were stalwarts on Killarney Legion teams of the era. But it was in May 1946 that Arthur E. O'Keeffe and Archie Cronin organised a team in Lissivigeen.

They played in the East Kerry Minor League that year. Most of the games they played were informal, organised by the primary schools on their own behalf. Lissivigeen, Tiernaboul and Knockanes would play each other home and away. That was the genesis of Spa, or at least the first tangible roots of a communal feeling on its way to being formalised.

Jamesie O'Donoghue's shop is only a memory now; it was on your left after the school. Jamesie's was a real country shop. You could literally buy anything there from cattle feed to cream cakes, and when times were tight there was never need for any long discussion about credit. Jamesie had an unusual sense of humour.

Every child in the neighbourhood hoped to be sent to Jamesie's for an errand – usually a bottle of milk or a box of matches.

He'd ask you a gentle riddle such as how to spell 'sciorthán' (bloodsucking ticks – every child was used to them over the summer and they were a regular annoyance but not dangerous). It didn't matter whether you got it right or not – I'm not so sure that Jamesie knew or cared that much – but he would always give you a penny bar for your efforts. And it isn't a childhood memory that makes me call them 'bars' rather than sweets; they were about two inches long and you could chew on them for hours.

On your right now as you go down the Pike Hill used to be Jack Moynihan's 'flat field'. Past that, and past the Pike Wood itself (a beautiful and short woodland walk now, with a mass rock from penal times in the middle of it – it's worth a stop along the way), Donie's Tiernaboul neighbour John 'Dunn' O'Donoghue had a garage.

On plenty of summer evenings, and more than a few winter ones, John 'Dunn' would bring a bunch of lads down from Tiernaboul, Knockmanmagh, and Knockeragh, gather up a couple more from 'The Island' (Ballyspillane) along the way, and play football in that field. They were purely informal games, but hugely popular. Other venues were Owen O'Keeffe's field down at the White Bridge or the Gravel Pit in Tiernaboul.

'Sweeney's gravel pit... it was small, but adaptable all year round,' remembers Donie. 'It was that bit small, but it kept us going... we played football, but with compromise rules. It was our meeting place.'

The games were hugely popular.

Girls didn't play – this was rough and tumble.

You might want to stop at the Killarney Heights Hotel for a cup of tea. The Riordans are the proprietors now; Bernie has been a long stalwart sponsor, and at several times manager, of the Spa team. While Bernie ran the hotel it was a great meeting place for Spa players and supporters. He was a good businessman and his retirement was a great loss to the area. The Coopers, a well-known Killarney family, had the Heights before the Riordans, when Donie was growing up. The watermill at the other side of the hotel was a well-known landmark up until fairly recent times.

Let's leave the Heights.

You are passing Daly's supermarket on your right now – it was founded on car sales when they were becoming more affordable in the 60s to the middle class. They have sponsored Spa teams for decades.

Turn right at Curtin's Cross, named, of course, for the Curtayne's. The last of them emigrated to America long ago, with the land around here being purchased by the Kelly Cronins. It was all farmland back then. Patsy Cremin, a vice-president of Spa and president of Kerry Coiste na nÓg (the juvenile section, formerly Bórd na nÓg) lived on Park Road into town which is to your left as you approach the roundabout. When he was growing up, there were three houses between there and the Railway Bridge at the edge of town. Now there are hundreds, including several housing estates.

We aren't turning left, nor are we going straight on over the by-pass that would lead you onto either the Ring of Kerry or towards Limerick. No, we are turning right at Curtin's Cross, past what used to be Cronin's shop – the Cronins are a great Spa family; one of them, Michael is the current chairman. Archie Cronin was a stalwart of Spa, while Pat Cronin was centre-back on the first ever recorded Spa team in 1942.

On your left now is the Pretty Polly Factory. Once, it was an important industry, employing several hundred people in manufacturing hosiery.

Turn left at the next roundabout.

On your right is Ballyspillane housing estate. I remember walking through those farm fields on my way to work at my first job; almost overnight in 1979 it seemed to change from rural to urban, and Killarney is still expanding in this direction.

Left and onwards.

This was woodland on your left; by the time you are reading this, new houses will be springing up in response to demand. Donie would cycle this road on his way to school when he first went to secondary school and know every human habitation that he passed along the way. That was then; this is now.

The population has quadrupled long since and motor cars, a rarity then, are a danger to cyclists now.

Further up, the road climbs all the way up from Killarney town – Donie was a lot quicker cycling to school than coming home from it! On your right is the Ballyspillane Industrial Estate. It was built as a part of the industrial expansion of the 1970s, Jack Lynch continuing the industrial and social revolution of Seán Lemass, and it worked.

The Post Office, Eircom, and Tricel International are some of the big employers here. Killarney is justly famous for tourism, and it puts dinner on a lot of tables, but a service-based industry like tourism is a very delicate egg if you only have one basket. The Industrial Estate doesn't make headlines, but it makes a difference.

Not to us.

We are driving past the entrance, only just past it.

There's a turn now to our right, and that's the road that we are taking. This is the heartland of Spa. These are Donie's roots.

He's been fairly quiet so far while I point out the landmarks on the way. He has been driving – he is a very good driver, but there's a lot of traffic on the Cork Road (it's an arterial national route) and Ballyspillane has a big population now. Donie has to keep his eyes on the road.

This road is that bit smaller and narrower, a country road. It's certainly not a boithrín ('bothar' is 'road, and 'in' is a diminutive suffix – a boithrín wouldn't have tar). This was a well-travelled road, but it was built when horsepower was meant to be taken literally.

Donie drives it easily; he knows every slight twist and turn here. *Knows the road?* He came put a name on virtually every tree and stone. Certainly, he knows the houses.

'PAST CRONIN'S IS O'Donoghues. They had the first radio in the area. The first All-Ireland final that I listened to was the famous 1947 final in the Polo Grounds... Michael O Hehir pleading for a bit more time to finish the broadcast... we were in a bigger panic than he was!

'Thady O'Sullivan's was another great meeting house. That was where I first heard Oliver Goldsmith's poetry.

'Thady Carthy lived there. A great character, witty and a friendly word for everyone. A lovable rogue.

'The house there is John 'Dunn' O'Donoghue's. He had the garage in Lissivigeen. Actually, if you took the boithrín there past John Dunn's, it would take you all the way down to Lissivigeen in a straight line.

'An uncle of John Dunn's lived in a small cabin there at what we called Phil's Haggard... it's gone now. I remember him telling me as an old man that the first time Phil wore shoes was the day he got married – and he spent as much of the day admiring his new shoes as his new bride. Phil was a cottier. There's a certain sadness to it all – a lot of landless families here who relied on farm labour for work simply died out in the years after the famine and later.'

The young people weren't staying – what was there to stay for? And the old people had nowhere to go and no way to get there anyway.

'If you look around here, you can see spectacular views... down over all of Killarney, with the lakes and the mountains in the distance. But look at it from a farmer's perspective – see all the rushes sprouting around the edges of the fields?

'Any farmer has his work cut out to make a living on ground like that. All coarse meadows... hopeless for hay.'

'Up top here, Fitzgeralds, and on the other side was Liam Browne. Just before Brownes was John Herlihy's house. Like my father, he had emigrated to the US, to Pittsburgh, and came back.

He had a radio – the sight of him cycling home from town on a September Saturday with the wet battery up on the bike was a sure sign that there was a game on the next day.

'There was huge anticipation of matches broadcast in the pre-television days. Wireless batteries were saved for the broadcasts, the house with a wireless set was the focal point in the local community. Neighbours gathered to hear the broadcasts and the one voice was Michael O'Hehir's... he was the eyes for thousands, his descriptions always colourful and unique... his identification of players instant.

'The excitement of the game was perfectly captured in his voice.

'The tension was unbearable.

'Just below Brownes is a left there. This is where my own parents lived and where I grew up. You are getting right into the heartland of Spa now. That's the Mission House on our right.

'Jimmy Culloty lived there. He was on the first Spa team... a good footballer. I played a lot of cards in that house.'

Thirty-one or 45 was and still is the game played around here. A player in Spa could be forgiven for missing a score in a big game of football, or getting a talking to from a referee, and certainly missing training if harvest or the bog was involved... but the eejit that trumps his partner's card will find no mercy this side of Heaven in Spa.

'Past Cullotys is Sweeney's gravel pit. That was close to hallowed round, young lads were playing football there since long before Spa had a team. Gravel ground, you see.

'It would hold up in bad weather – it was the only ground around here that could be played on constantly. You could play all year round... and we did. Outside of farm-work, what else would we have to do?

'On the right now is Fleming's house. Tom Fleming was another great character... he stood at 6'5". You'd spot him in any crowd. That was a strong Republican house.

'Jimmy was a training officer of the IRA in Killarney; he was interned in the Curragh in the 1930s. He was the best footballer in the family, one of the best footballers around. He played with Legion before Spa was founded – Paddy Fleming, his brother, was a founder of Legion, and Jimmy won a county championship with them in 1946. Dermot, a lifelong friend, played as well. His grandnephew Diarmuid is a hugely respected journalist and researcher now with the BBC and Al Jazeera.'

'David and Paddy Fleming were active in the IRA in the North; Patrick was on the IRA Army Council, and David was imprisoned in Crumlin Road in Belfast. David was the youngest of the boys, and had a hard time of it and suffered brain damage due to ill treatment.

'David was involved in the planning of an escape attempt – three lads got away, but David, Joe Cahill, and John Graham were caught in the act. Prison conditions deteriorated fast after that, to an intolerable degree. David went on hunger strike twice – he spent longer on hunger strike than any other prisoner. In the end, his mind almost broken and his body reduced to a skeleton, he was released on compassionate grounds by the Unionist government in 1947. It was a big national talking point by then – 50 British MPs had signed a petition calling for his release.'

Spa, like Sliabh Luachra (a cultural hinterland of East Kerry/North West Cork) clung onto gaelic traditions of language, music and dance much longer than more urban areas of Ireland. There was, perhaps, as much obduracy as pride in it at times. It was also less influenced by economic influences than Killarney town – tourist money was good when it came to landed estates and lake views; less so where people eked out livings from small farms.

Regardless of the how or why, this was republican territory all the way in the War of Independence.

That wasn't just lip service, either.

David Fleming wasn't the only active participant from around here and there was a tacit approval in republican activities in households that didn't play an active part. The community around here was firmly on one side, and it wasn't the Dublin authorities.

A young Donie couldn't have been unaware of the history, even if he had wanted to. Just past McGillicuddys, up to the left, is a spot that he, like the Flemings before him, would pass every day when walking to and from school. It isn't marked; it doesn't need it. It was indelibly inked in the mind of everyone in the locality ever since 1923.

'You can't quite see it today,' says Donie, matter-of-factly. 'Just up there was an old dugout with an iron roof. That was where they captured Stephen Buckley, Dan Donoghue and Tim Murphy. They were on the run, having been fighting the Free State around Killarney.'

Was their capture in such an isolated area just unlucky, and in fact fateful coincidence or was it something more sinister? No one knows or has ever known; that is the grotesque nature of any civil war. They were captured, beaten, tortured, and finally taken to the Countess Bridge on March 7, 1923. They were ordered under rifles to move some stones... which had been wired with explosives. Those who survived the initial explosion faced further detonations before being machine-gunned... Tadhg Coffey survived, though badly wounded, and managed to reach Jack Moynihan's house. A similar massacre occurred in Ballyseedy in Tralee, with nine men blown up and only one, Stephen Fuller, surviving.

It only counts as history now, and was glossed over more often than not; a young Ireland took great pride in saints and scholars of centuries ago but didn't want to risk awakening any of the more recent ghosts.

STORIES GROW IN the telling around here.

The oral traditions are still very strong. Sure, what else would people be doing?

Tim Horgan's *Fighting for the Cause: Kerry's Republican Fighters* is probably the best source on these and other tragedies. Tim's father, Declan was one of the earliest founders of Kerry Bórd na nÓg in the late-60s, an initiative promoted by a man Donie would come to know well, county board chairman Dr Jim Brosnan.

Dr Jim Brosnan's father was Con Brosnan of Moyvane, and he was one of the greatest Kerry footballers of his day, a key component in midfield alongside Bob Stack (another who returned from the United States) of Kerry's first four in-a-row from 1928-31. When the Civil War was still blazing across Kerry, and the deaths of Buckley, Murphy, and Donoghue were still fresh in people's minds, Con Brosnan, a Free State captain, brokered a truce that allowed John Joe Sheehy, Commander of the Tralee battalion of the IRA, to emerge out of the crowd at the start of the 1924 Munster final and join the team.

Kerry won that All-Ireland. Sheehy would later return the gesture by nominating Brosnan as the 1930 Kerry captain – not all of Sheehy's republican friends in Tralee approved, but it helped reconciliation in a county where the wounds were fresh and bleeding.

'You are past Tiernaboul now and into Knockeragh. But, actually, Tiernaboul school is of note... it was opened on April 1, 1838. Twenty years later, in 1958, the

District Inspector of National Schools visited the school. He reported that the land holdings in the area were small and barren, and that the school was situated in a 'wild' neighbourhood… it was a curious and gratuitous report.

'The school closed in 1912… a new school opened on the same site.

'A lot of the area is changed now from when I grew up here. Up there is the creamery; that was a focal point of any community back then. The Morris' lived on the left, great Spa people. Just there is Donie O'Leary's house. Donie was very much a part of the heart and soul of Spa all his life. He was one of those who founded the Spa club in 1948, in the Casey's home.

'Paudie Casey, Pat's son, farms there now, His brother Mike lives nearby, preferring life in Knockmanagh than San Francisco. Two others, Denis and Maurice, still live in San Francisco.

'Connie Cronin and I were in Tiernaboul school at the same time. He loved music, and football and dance. He was great fun, and had a great sense of humour, but was as hard as nails… he died too young, but the stories and memories remain.'

The road moves on, narrow enough and hedge-lined, but with a modern surface. This road pre-dates cars; a lot of Irish roads do, but it can handle its fair share.

'You're in Knockmanagh now. You can see where some fields have been drained for farmland, but you'll drain no land forever.' Donie was a farmer's son, never a farmer, and I'm not sure that he even realises that he sees this land with his father's eyes.

Real nostalgia doesn't need to be layered with sentiment. He has travelled all over the world and he has lived for many years in Tralee in a great community. But there is a part of his soul that has never really left his birthplace and homeland. I don't know; I think that might be true of all of us.

'That's Patrick Cahill's house on the right… great Spa people the Cahills, great story-telling people! Further on, there's another Cahill family… brothers Jimmy and John Joe were the Spa midfield from 1948 to '51. Jimmy's family, John, James and Willie were outstanding Spa players in later years.

'Mick Kearney lived in that house on the left. Liam Kearney, the Spa and recent Kerry midfielder now, is his grandson. Beside it is Carrolls. Just ahead of us, on the left again, is Denis Galvin's house.'

Technically we are on the cusp of Spa now, at the edge of Knocknahoe ('The Hill of the Yew' – though there are no yew trees around here anymore) and

Knocknaskeha ('The Hill of the Bushes' – and yes, that one is still perfectly apt!), or even a bit past it. This is Glenflesk ('Glenna na Fleisce'), a great club in its own right. If you haven't heard of Seamus Moynihan, John Crowley, Derry Crowley and other Kerry footballers from Glenflesk, why exactly are you reading this book? It was originally Headford GAA Club – we will speak more of Headford anon.

'The Regans grew up there in that house over there. All the Regans are big men – Jerome played for Legion, while Tim and Andy are both Spa. Tim played football for Kerry in the 70s, and might even have played a bit more but for his first love, basketball – he was a hugely respected Irish international.

'On the right is Raheen National School. That old ruin on the left hand side was the old school. My mother went to school there. Madge Cronin used to teach there.

'Up here is the Creamery Cross. If you turn left, you are on the road to Scartaglin. Down right is Barraduff. My memories of Barraduff go back to the mid-40s.

'Going there on Sundays to attend Mass in an old jaunting car, my Uncle Danny Bawn at the controls. After Mass, there was a visit to Murphy's pub. This was the home of Fr Gerry Murphy. For over 40 years he laboured in God's fields in the diocese of San Diego.

'Forty years or close to it, and so far away from the quiet of Barraduff, would make most American, or close to it. But he was first an Irishman, more so a Kerryman… and perhaps even more so again, a proud son of Barraduff and Sliabh Luachra.

'I've got memories also of another Murphy family from Barraduff, Tom and John. Due to a tragic car accident, John was a paraplegic for 40 years, but his courage and good spirits were an inspiration to us all. He loved gaelic football, and especially Kerry football.

'He was an example of the triumph of the human spirit.'

Not too much farther now. We'll stop here at Faha (The Fathach), and this is well worth a stop. You'll see the plaque fixed to the wall on your left.

"An Fhaiche (Faha)… Seat of Learning, Poetry, Music, and Hurling."

It doesn't tell you too much, does it? Well, in its hey-dey, there wouldn't even have been a plaque. Back in the 19th century, when the British Empire was bent on stamping out native Irish culture, this was one of the most famous of the places that defied them.

This was a hedge school. Cultural defiance needed a lot more than weapons or resentment to evoke freedom, and Faha was one of the greatest of places that supplied it.

'Eoghan Rua Ó Suilleabháin (1748-1784) taught here. One of the great Kerry Poets,' explains Donie. 'He was educated at the bardic school at Faha, where music and the classics were taught. He's buried in Muckross Abbey.

'Séafraidh Ó Donnchadha an Ghleanna would be another. Aogán Ó Rathaille (1670-1726) in particular was a notable character. In gaelic Ireland, he would undoubtedly have been a high-ranking bard among the McCarthy Mór family (rulers of this part of Kerry back then) but instead he was reduced to being a farm labourer. His poems are amongst the finest in the language, lamenting the decay of the old gaelic order. He was born in Scrahanaveal, and connected to the bardic school too.'

Ó Rathaille's poetry was particularly scathing towards Valentine Browne, a former benefactor – and make no mistake, Irish poetry in the bardic style could be absolutely scathing. Gaelic Ireland always valued words, and bards ranked high in society. For Ó Rathaile, the reduction in status and income from his expectations drew both his ire and his wit.

'Their work would almost certainly have been lost but for an tAthair Padraig Ó Duinnín... Fr Patrick Dineen. He was a Jesuit, who did a huge amount to preserve and translate a lot of Irish writing. He was an editor, author and compiler... he was born in 1860 in Carn, in Rathmore. He attended a school in Meentogues which was built from stones taken from the ruined house of Aogán Ó Rathaille. Mentioned in *Ulysses*, he produced the great Irish dictionary.'

Donie shows me a book that he has. An original printing of that self-same dictionary. That would be special in itself, but this one is a lot more special than that.

'Máirtin Ó Cadháin had these and used them to teach Irish when Republicans were interned in The Curragh. There were only three or four copies in all. This one was John Joe Sheehy's.'

It's a hard-back copy, of course, and it's covered with green cloth, which was part of a prison blanket. 'They wanted to preserve the few copies that they had,' Donie says, matter-of-factly, 'so they made covers out of the blankets for them.'

DONIE HAS COMPLETED his drive.

But he feels that his words, and his directions, have been somehow incomplete. He produces an article written by his late friend Dermot Fleming, who left Tiernaboul and lived in Dublin most of his life.

It was written in 2000, and recalls happy days growing up in Spa. 'The essence of where we are,' insists Donie.

Donie would like it shared.

It is titled 'The Theatre of Dreams'.

If it's drama you want brother, then here it is!'

The commentator, the late Paddy O'Leary back from his sojourn in Australia.

The location, Scotts Field, Tiernaboul.

The year, circa 1957.

Scotts Field, as it was known locally, had passed into the benign ownership of Jack Doherty RIP and become the Theatre of Dreams for the male population of Tiernaboul and its hinterland.

This was the era of Miss Courtney's Chester Cakes, Mick Spillane's hobnailed boots. The County Council and the Forestry paid 5.25 pounds for a five and a half day week, and 4.80 pounds took you from Killarney to Paddington, via Rosslare, and the chance of starting with Murphy at three pounds a day.

It was a victory to get to secondary school and a miracle if you went any further. A gay man was a man who went to the races on a wet July day with two fields of hay down and a ten bob note in his pocket. Partners played 31 and didn't usually share a domicile and preferring girls to football was regarded as a form of social deviancy.

Those of us, who in the latter stages of primary school made our way to the Monastery, found our rustic stoicism tested to the limit by Brother Emmanuel and Brother Philip. Vocational guidance was pragmatic – if not academically inclined, you were advised to 'put a shilling in the spade fund'. 'Watch your books you'll end up in the County Home' was one reminder from the mouth of my Uncle Tommy Fleming. Given the present rate of inflation the spectre of the County Home hasn't yet receded.

Urban and rural relations were not always harmonious. Being labelled by the townies led to many a skirmish on the Park Road, and made the journey to Curtin's Cross a hazardous one. Who remembers McGurran the rabbit trapper and his problem with the Tiernaboul super rabbits – who extricated themselves Houdini-like from the most modern of traps.

The Purcells, a showbusiness family, were yet another colourful addition to the local scene. Their excursions to town on piebald ponies were viewed with approbrium by the more respectable locals and no doubt contributed to their premature departure.

September 1953 at least 30 neighbours gathered at John O'Brien's to listen to Armagh V Kerry, adults in the kitchen and youngsters in the yard. Armagh got a penalty and the silence could be heard at the Friary.

McCorry shoots wide, and the following day the Independent proclaims 'Bouquets for Lyne, Sheehan and Brosnan'. The Kerry half-forwards carried the day. Morgan, Bratten and McKnight kept a grip on our full-forward line.

By the late 50s progress for the Spa club looked anything but bright. Ageing and emigration had weakened the great teams of '48 and '49 and the whole future of the club seemed problematic. Nationally, emigration was running at 80,000 per annum and the Spa area was no exception to the national trend.

Timmy Joe O'Sullivan was the custodian of the club jerseys which reputedly he kept in a canvas bag under his bed, from which they were to emerge Phoenix-like in the 60s. The story has a poetic ring which grows more authentic with the passage of time.

The foundation of the Naomh Mhuire juvenile club in 1954 by Tadhg O'Sullivan was to prove a crucial turning point in the history of the Spa club. It was to give the boys who had started to congregate in numbers in Doherty's field a competitive outlet and rebuilt the link with Muckross and Lissivigeen which had been weakening rapidly. The first set of Naomh Mhuire jerseys were purchased from Seán Óg Ó Ceallacháin's shop in Dublin for the princely sum of 11 pounds.

The field in Tiernaboul had a billiard-like surface and was 'all-weather', not surprising, as it was adjacent to a sandpit. It had two problems – namely length and width.

Taking a leaf out of Joe Stalin's book, whose dictum was 'If circumstances and dogma come into conflict, circumstances will have to change', it was decided that if the field couldn't be changed, the game would have to change.

Thus was born the first set of compromise rules.

We didn't have the nomenclature but we certainly had the idea. Given the present state of the game, we are only a special congress away from the oval ball.

From the mid-50s on, games were played on most summer evenings with the exception of Sundays when, if we had the eight pence for the pit, we made our way to Tom Cooper's emporium on the east avenue. Marcus O'Neill, the great South Kerry and county goalkeeper, was a special hero and he had a few dangerously accomplished apprentices who added spice to the proceedings.

On Sundays, games started at midday after last Mass, numbers began to swell, augmented by younger devout Mass-goers and later in the afternoon by more seasoned campaigners, nicely oiled, having spent an hour or two in Gandhi's or Pat O'Meara's. Bikes were thrown against ditches, bicycle clips were removed, ends were tucked into socks, body coats were divested and battle was joined.

Age or ability were no barrier.

Often Deros green Anglia was stopped and the passenger list scanned for suitable participants. Another anomaly was the absense of a referee. This was an exercise in self-regulation, so beloved nowadays by the professional bodies and multi-nationals – another first for Spa!

Fierce though the physical exchanges were, more damaging again were the metaphors and epigrams that peppered the Tiernaboul air. Some of these are best left to an oral hearing before an invited audience in Jimmy O'Brien's in College Street. 'Were they bad?'

'Bad? The 15 of them together wouldn't pull a cow out of a boghole.'

Time rolled on, and the boys of the 50s became the men of the 60s. Of the team of 1966, Tom and Jack Morris, Denny and Johnny Doolan, Johnny Batt Cronin, Paddy Dennehy, Fr Michael O'Donoghue, Donie O'Sullivan, Brian Fenton, Seanie Moynihan, John Dunne O'Donoghue RIP, Mick Kissane and Timmy Joe RIP were all regulars on the Elysian field of the 50s.

Emigration robbed the team of Tim O'Sullivan, Patsy Kissane, Jer Joe O'Sullivan and Michael Morris – all accomplished players. The scene in Spa would have been replicated in many parts of rural Ireland in the 50s and 60s. But few of them produced a player of the half-century.

Immensely improved economic circumstances, widespread access to second and third level education, and demographic shifts, have changed the texture of life in the Killarney area beyond recognition. These changes have created new challenges and opportunities for the club.

Let us hope that some of the idealism, courage, gaiety and rebelliousness that characterised the Spa area still remain.

The centenary of the club is only 42 years away.

There are cups to be won. Sam Maguire to be brought home and stories to embroider. But don't let those jerseys take refuge under the bed again, under any circumstances.

Donie's father Michael and his mother Catherine Murphy on their wedding day. And with his siblings John, Tim, Joan Maureen and Marian.

« CHAPTER 2 »

GAELIC FOOTBALL, ATHLETICS and rowing were the games they played. Handball, another gaelic game, was played in Killarney and all over Kerry, but it was in Tralee and Ballymacelligott that it really flourished. It didn't feature much in Spa until more recent years when All-Ireland champion handballer as well as Kerry junior footballer, Pa Murphy married into the club and introduced members to the joys of the sport. Anyone who is fit enough to play out a full game of handball, a very energetic game, will last a game of football too!

It would simply be unthinkable to play any other sports. Time, and an independent sense of a national identity, have diluted earlier views of soccer, rugby, and to a much lesser degree, cricket. That was the most popular sport in Ireland before independence; Cusack was one aficionado. George Bernard Shaw, the great playwright, was another. He wrote, not without affection, that *cricket is a game played by 11 fools and watched by 11,000 fools,* while a prominent US journalist once noted *The English are not a very spiritual people, so they invented cricket to give themselves some idea of eternity.* To be fair, in the rough and tumble game of caid and the early days of gaelic football, with the uncompromising nature of the games, a few players came closer to eternity than they might have expected!

Camogie was popular up until the 1930s for girls, with Dr Crokes having a strong team in Killarney. Even in the 1950s, women playing sports were expected to wear long trousers. Skirts were unthinkable! Ladies football only arose in the

1970s and has risen like a phoenix ever since. Anyone talking about the delicate sensibilities and shy nature of women simply hasn't met any. The old euphemism has it that, 'horses sweat, men perspire, but ladies merely glow'. All I can say is that if any ladies started glowing around the Killarney area, you'd call for both a priest and a doctor, just in case.

Coursing was and is huge in North and West Kerry, but wasn't a big thing around Killarney. Though hurling was played in Killarney, that has always been much stronger in North Kerry and in outposts around Kenmare and Kilgarvan than anywhere else in Kerry – I have heard speculation that it is because of the quality and availability of landlords' fields, but can't confirm that.

Rowing in Killarney is the oldest sport of them all. Races were regularly held on the Lakes of Killarney in the 1700s. The first recorded regatta was organised by the Lough Lein Rowing Club in the early 1800s. The various town trades were strongly represented, with bakers, carpenters, grocers and drapers racing each other. Aghadoe and Muckross (Muckross was active as far back as the 1600s and may well be Ireland's oldest sports club) regularly travelled to regattas in Kenmare, Templenoe, and Cork City.

In 1847, at the height of the famine, a regatta was held on the Lakes of Killarney, from O'Donoghue's Prison to Darby's Gardens. The regatta was one of the biggest social events of the year and still is to this day.

In Killarney, the Cricket Field (by Flesk Bridge, almost opposite the Gleneagle Hotel) was the epicentre of field sports. Horse-racing started in Coolcorcoran in 1822 before the Bunrower course was built. Horses and hounds were key pastimes of the respectable rich. All of these were more for the gentry and the professional classes than for ordinary people, though.

Athletics was much more accessible, even though the events were confined to strictly amateur competitors (i.e. no prize money). Human nature being what it is, the likes of JP 'The Champion' O'Sullivan (who instigated the switch of Laune Rangers in Killorglin from a rugby club to a GAA one, Kerry's first superpower of the game) were well minded when they attended athletic events.

Golf was popular among the gentry – Killarney's golf course was private property of the Kenmares. In 1893, Killarney Golf and Fishing Club was founded with 40 members paying an annual subscription of 40 shillings. Although wage rates for agricultural and construction workers had risen since 1860 as a result of famine and emigration reducing supply, they were still only seventy-five percent of their English counterparts. Forty shillings? There weren't a lot of small farmers, labourers, or tradesmen rushing to take up golf.

BUT THE GAELIC revival and the achievement of independence meant that gaelic games was the sport for ordinary Irish people.

At the same time, soccer was an English game, not an Irish one. The workers on the Transatlantic Cable Company on Valentia Island from 1857 onwards (itself a historic achievement) were working-class Englishmen for the most part and loved the game.

There were challenge games between the visitors, including ships' crews, and the locals. However, it doesn't seem that locals played the game among themselves, and 'soccer' was a broad and undefined term almost synonymous with rugby or the Irish 'caid' at the time. In *Soccer in Munster: A Social History 1887 to 1937* by David Toms of UCC (published in 2015), Kerry doesn't get a mention. Soccer was almost non-existent in the county when Donie was growing up. Exceptions to the GAA's Rule 21 – the Ban – were rare and almost always involved rugby. As recently as 1938, the GAA had officially called on President Douglas Hyde to resign on the basis that he had attended a soccer match.

Basketball was relatively new in Killarney. Ben Campion (the Laois native who managed the Killarney minors to three county titles in-a-row at the start of the 50s) founded the first local basketball club in the town in October 1951. The first games were played in the old Killarney Town Hall (at the Market Cross in the centre of the town) and later the Parish Hall.

The famous Harlem Globetrotters played an exhibition match on an outdoor court at Killarney Racecourse in the mid-50s. Basketball continued to grow during that decade with the Town Hall hosting the All-Ireland Championship finals in October 1955, and a proper Town League was established as the new sport of basketball flourished in Kerry.

Basketball was very much a town-based game, though, and didn't have much impact on outlying areas such as Tiernaboul.

Rugby was played, and in fact the first recorded game of rugby in Killarney was in January 1888. Dr William O'Sullivan played Munster Senior Cup and had lined out for Ireland in 1895, as well as playing football for the Dr Crokes club. He was a

Free State Senator in the first Seanad in 1922 (his house was burned down by the IRA during the Civil War). Rugby was tolerated in a way that soccer wasn't.

THESE WERE ALL things that Donie would have known as simple facts as a child without understanding them. You played and followed gaelic football because... well, it was your sport. Donie's fond childhood memory of John Herlihy making his way back to Tiernaboul on a Saturday with the wet and dry batteries for the radio – it always meant that the community would gather at Herlihy's the next day to listen to Michael O'Hehir extol the deeds in Croke Park at whatever match was on.

'I can still see John Herlihy, I can picture him in my mind's eye... coming up the road on his bicycle on a Saturday before the game... with that wet battery on the handlebars.'

In time, Donie himself would be in Croke Park playing in green and gold, and families at home would be listening in to his deeds, or watching on from afar. He knows that both victory and defeat washed over his own parents. His father died in 1993, short of his 90th birthday; his mother passed in 1999, at 91 years of age. 'My footballing days with Kerry never troubled them, I hope. They would have enjoyed it to a certain extent, but they didn't go to Croke Park. My father had gone in 1938... and he might have gone up there once more after that.

'My father only played a little football. I'd imagine they would be as happy as any parents are in seeing their son playing for a county, but they would never indulge themselves. I was grateful for that, and my father would never talk much at all about a game afterwards. Only a little bit... we didn't need to talk about football games more than that.'

Donie does recall sitting down and listening to the 1947 All-Ireland final, the game coming the whole way from the Polo Grounds in New York, where Kerry battled it out against Cavan. He remembers being in the company of his father and his elder brother.

'That was a kind of treat, and he also brought us to the county final in 1950. I was 10, and setting off on a great adventure... the three of us again. We got the train to Tralee to see the game. It was a Killarney team playing, that included the Spa club. The captain of the team was Maurice Casey, and Donie O'Leary played aswell; both really good neighbours and friends. The game was a draw... I can still see it clearly.

Surprisingly, neither man was on the team for the replay, which Castleisland won.'

Even the few people who had no great interest in football, lovable eccentrics that they were, would come for the social gathering at Herlihy's and the banter – with the occasional epithet and pronouncement from local sages. Padraig 'PF' Foley in *The Kerryman* was required reading in every household on Thursdays – any prior judgements of the game was mere speculation, PF's word was law.

'We would read every single thing he wrote, but we would also read the paper from front to back. We would never miss anything that was happening. But PF's opinions would get everyone talking.'

Reading more, and learning more, were just as important in the O'Sullivan household. 'The reason my father wanted to get a place here, I think, is so that we would have the opportunity of attending secondary school in Killarney. He had enough of an education to know how little he had, of how much he had been deprived of a greater, more formal education through his younger life.

'And, after spending so many years in Boston, he was still aware what Yankee New Englanders – WASPS – thought of the 'mere Irish'.

'I can see why that was important to him. Everyone was merely surviving here when he was a boy. As we get older, we realise more and more, and understand more the sacrifices our parents made for us.'

Donie always loved reading.

He feasted on his first books.

'I would read anything… any paper or book I could get my hands on. There was so little at times, all the same. The first book I got in St Brendan's was *Kidnapped…* Robert Louis Stevenson. We were given the book as part of our course in English.

'It was like Christmas morning for some of us.

'I could not put it down… every page would come alive. It was like listening to the radio, the picture was in the mind's eye. It transported us out of our lives and far away… to Scotland and the isles, and the Jacobites, and Culloden.

'It was wonderful. I would read it every night, even though there was no electricity… till the end of the oil lamp.' Which brings Donie to another memory, of a former great president of St Brendan's who taught the classics, Latin and Greek and English.

'He was a big man… grey hair, and he was with this young lad who had handed in a composition. And he announced, "Boy, why did you write only one page in your composition?" The boy replied the lamp quenched.'

Books brought Donie on a treasured path through his years of study as a young man, but also through his footballing days with Kerry he was never alone in having a good book in his hands. 'There were always a few readers on the team,' Donie admits. 'They wouldn't be talking very much about what book they were reading, but Michael Gleeson and Mick O'Connell were big readers… Micheal O Sé too.'

Donie and the magnificent O'Connell, and Gleeson, O Sé, Tom Long and John Culloty would become firm friends later in their lives, when all football matters were of another day.

'There were only a few years between us, but in the dressing-room we were never what you'd call big friends with Mick O'Connell… we were all in awe of the man! He was so talented, and so bright. We were in New York once or twice and got to know one another better on our travels, I suppose.

'We talk a couple of times most weeks, now… we talk about everything in life, which means we don't talk very much about football at all. You can play football with someone for years, but it is all about the person… not the footballer.'

If Robert Louis Stevenson was the first author to enliven the imagination of a young Donie, then Jane Austen was awaiting him when he entered Maynooth to study for the priesthood, to dampen the same mind. '*Persuasion*…!' he notes. 'It wasn't appealing. The writing was excellent, but if they'd thrown in something by Joyce, or Scott Fitzgerald?'

Donie would have preferred some classic *Gatsby*.

'Instead, we were reading about these people in these country houses in England. They believed it served a purpose, though the setting was far removed from the uplands of Tiernaboul.'

Of course, Donie the student was as afraid of Joyce as the next person, and the wonder and the doubt that fills an early reader when he picks up many of the works of the Dublin author. 'Someone gave me one of his books, and I read right through it, and then I needed to read everything he did.' Like the rest of us, he sought a helping hand from other authors, as he got to grips with *Ulysses*.

This was long after Donie O'Sullivan had left the confines of the dressing-room, and its time-consuming ways. He read Joyce, and was thrilled by Chekov. Actually, he admits to getting 'hooked' on the work of the Russian playwright.

This was during Donie's days in California with his family, when whole summers in the 1980s and 90s were devoted to teaching in San Diego.

In the university, he had access to free tickets for events and the theatre. 'The first time I went to *Uncle Vanya*, I couldn't believe the whole experience... I had to go the very next night to see it again.'

The great writers impacted on Donie, the footballer, but later in life he found time to revisit them all, at a more leisurely pace. 'Some of these writers, they might not mean very much to you when you are in the middle of a busy life... of football and family and work, but when you revisit them, later in life, you find an entirely different work.

'But I was always reading. As we prepared for the All-Ireland final in 1970, I remember... the week leading into the game can be slow and pain-staking. I came across the memoir of a man who had studied and taught at Maynooth College... *Reminiscences of a Maynooth Professor*. His name was Walter McDonald (1854-1920) from Mooncoin in Kilkenny.'

Not everyone's cup of tea, he agrees.

'I found it ideal for the week that in it!'

From *The Kerryman* to *Uncle Vanya*, with *Reminiscences of a Maynooth Professor* in between.

GAELIC FOOTBALL WAS as much a part of yourself as being Irish, or being Catholic... or being *Kerry*. It would only be years later, as an adult, that Donie was able to put that inarticulate but commonly understood certainty into words. He did so most famously at a lecture in New York University, at Glucksman House, where he said:

The English Public School (a private linguistic hypocrisy – they weren't for the public) students were prepared for the responsibilities of business and empire. Sport was also identified not only with character-building, but also the 'white man's burden'. The ideology of imperialism in England and elsewhere glorified the playing fields as the source of qualities essential to national greatness and martial success. The founder of the modern Olympic Movement, Pierre de Coubertin, attributed the imperial success of the English to the influence of the public schools.

These English public schools and the values they inculcated had their counterparts in Ireland. Cristóir Ó Floinn, in celebrating the centenary of the GAA, wrote the following poem acknowledging the GAA as Ireland's response to that indoctrination and subordination of Irish culture through sport.

> *When Irish schools were aping after*
> *Eton and Harrow across the water*
> *And pastimes for their pupils made*
> *Which English public schoolboys played*
> *'Twas then, a hundred years ago*
> *A man from Clare arose to show*
> *That Ireland was, as Tandy said,*
> *'A most distressful country', dead*
> *To honour, soon the bells might toll*
> *For a nation that had sold its soul.*
> *A teacher, Michael Cusack knew*
> *The lesson learned at Waterloo:*
> *'My victory,' said Wellington*
> *'On Eton's Playing Fields was won'.*

A third of Wellington's forces during the Napoleonic Wars were Irish – it was poverty, not patriotism, that made them soldiers and, all too often, cannon fodder. The survivors, of all nationalities (though the idea of nationhood was still subsumed in imperialism around the globe) were not treated kindly by the Empire they had saved. Wellington himself was born in Dublin but was resolutely English and a monarchist – 'Being born in a stable,' he drily observed, 'Does not make one a horse'.

A fledgling Ireland had an almost instinctive resistance to anything English. None of the kids that Donie played with could have explained it. They just played football because… well, because it was the game they played. Games were usually informal – juvenile development in the GAA was sporadic where it existed at all.

SPA'S FIRST PITCH as such (no club owned grounds at that time; it only became commonplace in the 1970s. In the hard 40s, any decent land was needed for farming) was loaned to them by Major McGillicuddy down by the White Bridge. In Tiernaboul, the games – almost always challenge games with neighbouring parishes – were played in Thade Joe's (O'Sullivan… though he was so well known the surname was unnecessary) field. Dan O'Leary's and John O'Keeffe's fields in The Park were also regular venues in later years. The Spa field, across the road from The Park, was purchased in 1974 from the O'Keeffe family.

Coaching was simply playing with or against older lads – the very best kind of coaching, when all is said and done. Later, Lissivigeen NS schoolteacher Tadhg O'Sullivan, helped by Timmy Joe O'Sullivan and Patsy Lynch of Sheheree (Paudie Horgan's house now), organised a parish league for schoolchildren, with an amalgamation of the Spa schools (Tiernaboul, Lissivigeen, Anablaha and Loreto) lining out as Scoil Mhuire.

The Master (who had played for Kerry, Dublin, Meath and Wicklow in his prime and would later be chairman of both Spa and East Kerry) and Timmy Joe knew their stuff and had a willing audience. Among them were the O'Sullivans – young Donie was game, but small.

IRISH HAD BEEN almost wiped out as a language but was making a government-sponsored revival in schools. It lived on in everyday language. Hiberno-English was a dialect that fell a bit short of combining two languages but did incorporate elements of both. It was especially strong in Kerry.

A bundle of sticks for the fire was a gabháil (handful) of cipíns (cipíní – sticks or matches). Nawshalling was the bawling of a child (cnáimhsealaí – grumbling or whining).

An amadán was a fool, no great harm in him but you wouldn't want him for a workmate all the same. A lúdramán was worse, a foolish, lazy, eejit.

Comhar was when neighbours grouped to work together for the common good; it has been replaced now with meitheal, which originally meant a group of labourers for hire.

A suicín was a favourite calf (suicín – a small suckler). A súgán was technically a rope made of hay or straw, but it meant a chair with that type of seat, which were common. The Súgán Earl of Desmond, James Fitzgerald, had been so-called because he had been appointed by his rebel ally Hugh O'Neill, and not by the far away Queen Elizabeth – her hand was stronger, though, and the 'Earl of Straw' died in London's infamous Tower.

M'anam dan Diabhal (name of the devil) was a common epithet and carried no real sting.

It was expressive, not vulgar.

'Yerra' or 'dhera' is probably the most clichéd example of Kerry speech. It's a way of downplaying significance. Saying 'yerra' at the start of a sentence means that you have no strong opinion on the subject. Kerry footballers say 'yerra' during match interviews, but they don't mean it.

Big highlights were the regular and informal dances (musicians were highly prized; Spa is beside the great cultural outpost of Sliabh Luachra, where Kerry tunes and dances can trace their unique heritage back through centuries). They were mostly in houses; dancing at the crossroads was much rarer than De Valera's aspirations imagined.

Most people unthinkingly assume that GAA clubs are defined by their success or otherwise of their senior team on the playing field. Nothing could be further from the truth. That is mistaking the flagship for the fleet.

Dancing and drama permeate every GAA club. Scór, the cultural competition that includes Irish dancing, set-dancing, ballad-singing, Irish music, quizzes based predominantly on Irish culture and the GAA, and novelty act, is as much a part of the GAA as the football and hurling games.

Drama is a part of Irish culture – the likes of Beckett, Shaw, Wilde, Synge, Friel and, of course, John B. Keane are pioneers as well as heirs to that tradition. A lot of GAA clubs raised funds by staging plays – Spa was one such.

During the world war – sorry, the 'Emergency'– hackney driver Tim McCarthy was one of the few who had a petrol ration. One night he was bringing a party back from a concert at which the song *Noreen Bawn* had featured, when Paddy O'Leary had the idea of composing a play based around the song. The eponymous heroine Noreen is a beauty who emigrates to the US and returns home to her broken-hearted mother and dies.

The play was organised by Paddy's brother, Donie with the O'Learys and the Caseys prominent, and Dan O'Donoghue on the accordion and Joan Murphy singing. It was initially performed in Casey's house and then in the school, with Fr Bob Murphy's permission.

The troupe of wandering minstrels then went travelling throughout East Kerry; people loved it, and Spa raised enough money for a set of jerseys.

ONE LEGACY OF Ireland having its own governance was a broader accessibility to primary education, and it was of a high standard.

After school in Tiernaboul, Donie was lucky enough to have the opportunity to go on to further education in St Brendan's College... known then and now as 'the Sem'.

Lads and dreams: Timmy McGillicuddy, Fr Tim O'Sullivan, Paudie Moynihan, Patsy Donoghue, Donie (front right), Mike (Steve) Healy , Johnnie McGillicuddy, John Joe Healy, Tadhg John Dunne, Michael Morris, Dermot Fleming and Ritchie Moynihan.

Donie (with Weeshie Fogarty, left, and Martin Scanlon) on one of his many visits to Glucksman House in New York where he has lectured on Irish history.

« CHAPTER 3 »

ONE OF THE most famous GAA nurseries in the country was St Jarlath's of Tuam. They have a whopping 12 Hogan Cups. Between 1946 and '67 they won six of those titles and lost another three finals. When you consider that there was no final played between 1949 and '56, that gives you a clear picture of how far ahead of anyone else they were in those times.

St Mel's of Longford were hot on their heels. In fact, St Mel's would defeat the Sem a few years after Donie had left the school during their run of four Hogan Cup finals in-a-row from 1961-64, winning in '61 and '62 and losing to Jarlath's the other two years.

St Brendan's in Killarney is right up there with these schools as a great GAA nursery. Tralee CBS could always go toe-to-toe with them, and Críost Rí of Cork gave them a lesson in the game on occasions.

But the Sem was always a boarding school, and a prestigious one. It was never an actual seminary, not even when founded by Bishop David Moriarty in 1860. It did involve early rising, daily Mass, and was by design as well as effect a junior seminary.

The president and most of the teaching staff were priests and many of the students went on to train for the priesthood.

The Sem is unquestionably a football school, though they encourage and participate in a wide range of sports.

DONIE DIDN'T GO there for the football, more so the education. Good job, too. Donie was a very good student. The one thing he wasn't very good at, really… was football. Donie was one of the smallest of the first-year in-take.

One of the first things that happened for the in-take into the Sem was a challenge game between the 'day boys' and the boarders. Donie actually played well on that occasion. Unknown to Donie, Fr Seán Quinlan, a teacher in the college and a renowned judge of good football (he would later be a Professor of Scripture at Catholic University in Washington, and later at Maynooth), observed that, 'the young lad on the right wing will be the best of them all yet'.

Fr Quinlan didn't miss much.

Boarders dominated the school population, of course. Day boys were almost like an incidental extra. Donie would cycle to school on an old high nelly bicycle. He was seldom late – on one of those big, single gear machines you could build up an awful lot of speed on the long gradient from the steppes of Tiernaboul to the lowlands of the Killarney Valley, and you'd whizz by a few exotic sights along the way!

The journey home was… well, Donie might not have had too much muscle behind his small frame the first few times that he did it, but he'd have felt every single one of them growing and more of them developing as his teenage years accelerated along that road.

The fact that he was a day boy might have played some part in his slightly slower development at football. The boarders played football virtually every day; it was a huge pastime for them. The boarders in the Sem almost had an indigenous culture, as all such institutions do, and it could be a tough place. Discipline was strict and an unspoken code of honour was demanded by and of fellow boarders.

The day boys were a part of the school, but not immersed in it. Donie liked the football fine, but it was the education that held his attention. He wasn't any fanatic about it, but he had always been an avid reader, and he blossomed in this environment. He won't say it, it isn't in his nature to do so, but he was obviously intelligent, very much so. He was also quiet and diligent.

'We studied the classics… Latin, Greek, Mathematics, English, Irish, History, Geography, Science. The idea of practical work-oriented subjects like metalwork or woodwork were not part of the curriculum.'

In some ways, the going was tough, but it was a comfortable and secure life in many respects too. A happy way to grow from boy to man – or at least, old enough and yet unwise enough to mistake oneself for full manhood. For Donie, it was early rising for the morning jobs on the farm, and then save enough time for a quick breakfast. Onto the bicycle and into the Sem. Then the cycle home, the couple of jobs that needed doing – on any farm there are always and ever a couple of jobs that need doing. Homework and supper. No one went hungry and no one shirked.

Donie kept playing football, but not in such a way that anyone was going to pay too much attention. He wasn't making the school teams and he wasn't standing out in the class leagues. He wasn't with any club, and there was no organisation of juvenile football in Kerry anyway. The juvenile championships were haphazard at best. It was more or less understood that lads learned by playing games among themselves, with the excitement of an occasional challenge match, or even a game or two in an East Kerry Championship. There was no structure for players like Donie to develop.

Every now and then a visionary would make a proposal at a county board or East Kerry meeting, but those sparks never became flames. Football was for grown men or prodigies, and young Donie O'Sullivan was considered neither.

'I was strong enough… I wasn't good enough,' Donie judges, rather harshly of himself. 'If you cycle in (from Spa to Killarney) on bad roads, about four or five miles… and back home again, and when you get home, you're working… working on the land, you won't have time to play too much football.

'I would have loved to play more at that stage, but I honestly thought I wasn't good enough. They had some very good teams in my years there, some outstanding footballers, and some of them, like Johnny Culloty, were good at every sport they touched. Johnny was an outstanding footballer, hurler, basketball player… and even in those early days, he always had a word of encouragement for others.

'I never felt under pressure as a student in St Brendan's. There were mostly priests teaching there in my time, and they were decent, good people. We would find out later that they weren't getting paid much either… most of the money in the school was used to keep the fees down.

'Going into Maynooth, I wasn't even on the class team. I wasn't known from St Brendan's, obviously, and maybe I didn't have the confidence in myself either.

'You can feel overawed at times in your life.

'I am always grateful to St Brendan's. We were so fortunate.'

Donie's brother Tim was already studying for the priesthood. But Donie had no particular plans for himself; the future would happen in its own time. Towards the end of his schooldays, his future started happening fast, maybe a bit too fast.

MAYNOOTH WAS WHERE young men went to study for the priesthood and minister in the home dioceses. Ireland was often identified by its Catholicism. The establishment were Protestant for the most part and remote from ordinary life. The power of the gentry was collapsing anyway as Britain's 'Golden Age of Parliamentary Democracy' gave way, under increasing commerce and industry, to a raw democracy.

The priests had been the champions of the Irish poor going back to penal times. They were invariably the most educated people in their communities and were confidantes, advisors, teachers and leaders. Not only that, but they were genuinely revered for their vocation and piety.

Becoming a priest was a great thing to aspire to and it was usually an honour to have a priest or nun in a family. Ireland had a curious role reversal to England's system of primogeniture. The eldest child didn't automatically inherit everything. In fact, the eldest child was the first from home, finding a job or an education or, plain and simple, a life that held a greater hope of a better quality of life.

Not all prospective priests went to Maynooth for their training, far from it. There were many religious orders and most had their own institutions. But Maynooth loomed large over them all.

St Patrick's College, Maynooth, was the obvious manifestation of Irish Catholicism to the English public. *The Times* in London had declared on April 17, 1843… *It's not Liberalism but Romanism which peel is forcing on the nation… It is not merely Popery; that is unpopular enough in England, especially Irish Popery: but it is Maynooth. It is a name and a thing above all others odious and suspicious to England.*

If you go to Maynooth University nowadays, you will find an ultra-modern set of facilities, a deservedly high academic reputation, and a full set of student support and social activities. It is one of Ireland's fastest growing universities and one of the most modern in outlook. It has come an awful long way from its origins as the Royal College of St Patrick in 1795.

Mind you, the Pope had called for Vatican II, which would shake the foundations of the Catholic Church but ultimately make them a lot stronger, and there were conflicting opinions within the church that were rarely revealed to the public. Maynooth was as conservative an institution as you could get, but the students couldn't but be aware that the church was changing. A much greater awareness of the increase in urban populations at the expense of rural ones meant that social life in general all over the world was changing and the church was getting ready to adapt to the new needs of their people, especially the poor.

Dr Liam Ryan, who would later become Professor of Sociology in Maynooth, was a strong commentator on the adaptation of the Government's Buchanan Report on Regional Planning in Ireland in 1969. Strangely, while the church's popularity and its political sway were beginning to decline, its influence at ground level in communities was actually deeper and more positive than before.

But those changes were only beginning in Donie's time in Maynooth. And in Maynooth, just as Donie was leaving, Tom Crowley landed in.

◄ ◄◆►►

TOM CROWLEY

It was a huge shock alright. In the early days, I was very friendly with Tony Barrett. He was the captain of the Kerry minors, but he missed the All-Ireland final. He came into Maynooth in 1963. The Kerry minors qualified for the All-Ireland final on the third Sunday of September. The Bishop of Kerry tried to intercede on his behalf, and so did the Kerry County Board.

The player who replaced Tony as captain was Tom O'Hanlon from Tarbert. He was studying for the priesthood as well, but in Kiltegan, which was a different religious order. The county board made the request of them and he was released to play, but with the strict provision that he was to be straight back to Kiltegan after the game.

Tom O'Hanlon left Maynooth, just as I did. He went to the Missions afterwards and became a great priest for the poor. Sadly, he died young.

My brother and I have talked about Maynooth with Donie. He has never expressed the slightest regret. We can't be condemning the people who put the regime in place. They meant well, always.

It was a very strange way of life, although we didn't know it at the time. There was

an enormous disconnect between professors, deans, and students. You never conversed...
it was unthinkable. You would never think of even greeting a professor when they
passed you in a corridor. There was very little friendliness.

There was one exception. Tom Fee always had a kind word for the students, he was
always approachable, and that meant a lot. Everyone who was there at the time has
great memories of him. (Tom Fee, of course, would become famous on a national level as
Cardinal Tomás Ó Fiaich, and would come to represent a kindlier, more approachable
face of Catholicism in Ireland)

My brother was two years older than me, but I could only meet him for an hour on
a Sunday. You could never be alone with a woman – that included your own mother. It
seems incredible now, but that was simply how it was at the time. You didn't question
it. Not at the time, anyway.

I left in 1965. I finished my degree in UCD. That was a lonely time. I have one
clear memory, though, that gives an idea of the people in Maynooth. I was walking
down O'Connell Street and I saw one of the Deans from Maynooth, Thomas Finnegan,
coming up against me. I nearly thought he'd cross the street – we would never have
spoken informally to each other. This time it was the exact opposite – he couldn't have
been nicer. He brought me for a cup of coffee and a sandwich, and tried to make sure that
I was doing okay. As he headed away, he gave me a tenner... and ten pounds was an
awful lot of money then. I was paying £1.45 a week for my flat; that'll give you an idea.

It made me realise that the way they treated us in Maynooth wasn't their own choice
or nature. They had great humanity and were rarely allowed to show it.

FR TOM LOONEY

I entered Maynooth in September of 1962, and Donie left in January of 1963. It was
a big shock to all of us. He was a Kerry footballer, so of course everyone knew who he
was. Mind you, the drop-out rate at that time was very high; only around a third of the
1963 entrants went on to become priests.

I was in the Sem in my Leaving Cert. Year when I was called into a meeting
with the President of the college, Monsignor John Moynihan. He talked to me about
the priesthood – it wasn't pushed on me at all but wasn't discouraged either. It was an
option and one I was interested in. I was asked what kind of priest I would like to be?

At that time, you had three options as a priest; you could become a Diocesan Priest
in Kerry, you could become a Missionary, or you could join the Franciscan Dominicans.

I opted for becoming a Diocesan Priest. Of course, on reflection, I and any of us were too young to be making a decision like that at such an age. The diocese would decide each year how many they would send from Kerry. In 1961 it was two, in 1962 it was four (three of whom went on to become priests), in my own year I think it was four as well.

It was expensive for families. A huge honour at the time, of course… but expensive. There was £95 pounds paid by a trust fund for trainee priests; the diocese would pay £95, and your family would pay £95, unless you were able to get a scholarship – it was a huge amount of money at the time.

It was a completely new and strange environment. The Rule of Division was very strict. Juniors (first and second years) couldn't speak with seniors (third and fourth years), and of course nobody could speak with the teachers. You had a separate house for sleeping in and a separate house for dining; there was no inter-action at all, really. You were allocated a number when you entered and those numbers beside you were your closest companions from start to finish. It was completely closed off from the outside world as far as we were concerned.

Don't misunderstand me. We weren't unhappy at all. They way of life may have been strict, but it wasn't a hard or cruel place at all. In fact, many of those who left the training or priesthood subsequently retain very fond memories of the institution itself. Former students who didn't go on to become ordained still print their own Maynooth Layman's Annual, Vexilla Regis and part of the reason that it is so popular is because it contains very little bitterness.

It's worth noting that Maynooth at that time was one of Ireland's foremost intellectual powerhouses. Remember that at that time very few people had the opportunity to go to third level, and the other national universities were more practically orientated. People made brilliant friends there; remember, you were living in close proximity with your peers and without outside influences, so we all formed very strong friendships that have lasted to this day. The way of life may have been strict, but there was no cruelty whatsoever.

Others will disagree with me, but I remember the food being of good quality. To be honest, I think it's a natural thing for people living in hospital or prison or the army or any kind of institution, to complain about the food. I remember it as being fine. Maynooth had its own farm. Students, teachers… everyone would work for one day in gathering in the potatoes and vegetables. You didn't have to, of course, you were quite free to spend the day in quiet contemplation. But virtually nobody did, for the simple reason that at the end of the day you had an enormous feast, a 'flame' we called it, and it was probably the biggest and best meal you would ever eat. For the likes of Donie, well used to farmwork, it would suit him down to the ground.

Maynooth was a very stimulating way of life. There was an equal emphasis on study – the standard of teaching and intellectual debate was captivating for all of us… prayer and sport.

Sport was absolutely huge. We played hurling and football almost every day and the inter-class leagues were taken hugely seriously. Of course, they were – Maynooth at that time took part in no outside competitions. There was no question of entering the Sigerson or Fitzgibbon or anything like that… it wouldn't have been considered appropriate for trainee priests.

You had a lot of great players in Maynooth; there were three Mayo minors in my own class. The standard was very high. Everybody knew Donie, of course, he was always an astonishing footballer and he stood out in any company.

◄◄◆►►

'I LIKED THE structure of Maynooth, the self-discipline,' Donie recalls. 'I made friends for life there.

'You studied, you slept, and you played sports.

'We didn't compete against other colleges, but inter-class competition was keen and full-blooded. I'd say we would certainly have won at least one Sigerson if we did. You were playing against a lot of the best inter-county footballers in the country every single day. You were eating a well-regulated diet and living a very ordered and structured life. Games were our only real recreational pastime and we loved them.

'I left in early 1963. It wasn't any one thing, but a lot of them.

'My faith is as strong as it ever was, but I was questioning myself. It is said that faith which does not doubt is dead faith. It is better to live with certain doubts than to live with doubtful certainties.

'I wasn't cut out for the priesthood, and the more I advanced, the more I realised it. It wasn't an easy thing to leave in those days, but it would have been the wrong decision had I stayed.'

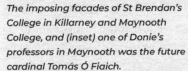

The imposing facades of St Brendan's College in Killarney and Maynooth College, and (inset) one of Donie's professors in Maynooth was the future cardinal Tomás Ó Fiaich.

« CHAPTER 4 »

KERRY FOOTBALL ACQUIRED almost mythical status right from its infancy, and people forget the reality behind the myth.

The gospel spread by Michael Cusack, a fire-and-brimstone preacher for his fervent cause, spread like wildfire. Cusack was a character, to say the least – the type of man who would deliberately and provocatively carry a walking stick that he named 'Bás gan Sagart' would often polarise opinion.

Then the GAA stalled and actually ran out of momentum – it's often forgotten nowadays how close it came to simply fading away in the early days.

Also, something that's completely taken for granted now, but is actually strange, is the fact that football rather then hurling dominates Kerry GAA. Think about it – it's the exact opposite in every other county in Munster.

Not only that, but Kerry had their first All-Ireland success in hurling, well before the football. Back in 1891, there were no inter-county teams. Participating counties would send their champion club to compete nationally, and in that year Ballyduff of Kerry beat Crossabeg of Wexford in the All-Ireland final.

There was a trick involved, mind you – that 'Ballyduff' team had several players who had joined them when their own clubs suddenly and mysteriously went defunct for the brief period of that campaign, before sparking back into life. There's rules and guidelines, and in Kerry like everywhere else, the lines can get blurred!

Laune Rangers, JP O'Sullivan's team from Killorglin, went close to winning football All-Irelands in those years, but never actually got over the line and would have to wait a full century for All-Ireland club success.

North Kerry was predominantly farmland, and the people and job opportunities were to be found in urban areas like Tralee. The Mitchels in Tralee were as strong and enthusiastic for hurling as football and enjoyed huge success in both codes by the 1920s, but football was the county's preference, arguably passion, by then.

IT WAS THE 1903 All-Ireland that sealed the deal.

It was actually played in 1905. Kerry played Kildare, and the game captured the imagination of the whole country. Kildare had already acquired the nickname of the Lilywhites and went so far as to whitewash their shoes. It took three games to separate them – one in Tipperary and two in Cork – and Kerry's triumph was soon to become legendary.

It was a windfall both financially and in publicity, and the GAA knew it. That was the 'Home' final, with London automatic qualifiers for the All-Ireland final in those days. Kerry beat that London team, captained by a certain Sam Maguire, and never looked back.

They won again a year later and never really lost the winning habit after that. Champions again in 1909, and they would have been favourites against Louth in 1910, but withdrew during a railway dispute.

Rebellion helped the GAA – and the GAA most certainly helped in the War of Independence. While the GAA was ostensibly neutral – and the struggle to keep it neutral when a strong cohort of its own membership didn't want to be is a long and interesting one of its own – the reality in Kerry is that the IRA and the GAA were intertwined. Austin Stack in Tralee and Dick Fitzgerald in Killarney were IRA commanders and Kerry footballers.

We weren't short of a small trace of arrogance, if we wanted to be fair about it. Wexford won four All Irelands in-a-row, but it hardly even needed to be said aloud that people in Kerry considered themselves otherwise occupied at the time with the War of Independence.

Dick Fitzgerald had captained Kerry to the 1913 and '14 All-Irelands, after all. By 1916, he was captaining a team in Frongoch prison in Wales, where he and many of the GAA's leading lights were interned.

Players were also interned in 1924, this time by an understandably nervous but vindictive Irish government. The Civil War was over, but civility between the opposing sides was very much at a high premium. When they were released, a challenge game was played between the former players who had been interned and the team who had replaced them.

The internees won and most regained their places… and Kerry regained their All-Ireland crown.

The football wasn't the talking point, though – that was IRA leader John Joe Sheehy on the run, with Free State captain Con Brosnan on the other side. Instead, under a carefully brokered truce, Sheehy emerged from the crowd to play the games and melted away back into it afterwards.

It was a definitive statement in its own right. Boiled down to its simplest form (and neither of these were simple men by any means) it said that in Kerry, football is more important than politics. All of that is history now, but gaelic football really is indelibly inked in Kerry's perception of its own identity. It transcends sport.

'The 1920s and 30s were decades of political turmoil in Kerry,' Donie observes, 'and gaelic games were a major factor in the eventual breaking down of the walls of hatred and bitterness. In the period 1924 to 1941, Kerry gained 11 senior football titles; this was achieved against a background of political tension.

'The uniting force of the GAA overcame political hatred. Republicans, Free State army officers, members of the Gardai Siochana, ex-internees and supporters of the Blueshirt movement played together on the same winning and losing teams.'

In 1926, Jack Murphy was brilliant as Kerry managed to get a draw against our great rivals Kildare again, despite the best efforts of Larry Stanley. He had died of pneumonia by the time Kerry won the replay.

Kerry's first four in-a-row team was considered the finest to ever play the game. Kildare lifted a brand-new trophy called after Sam Maguire Cup in 1928, but they didn't have it for long. Tralee was so strong by now that it split into three clubs. They still provided the backbone between them for a nigh invincible Kerry side.

The opening of Fitzgerald Stadium in May was the headline act in 1936. Dr Eamonn O'Sullivan's patients in St Finan's played a huge role in building it as part of their occupational therapy, an area in which the doctor was well ahead of his time. Kerry were unlucky to lose to Mayo in the semi-final.

It was five years now since they last lifted Sam Maguire.

Five whole years, and Kerry supporters were starting to feel it. They met Laois in the semi-final in 1937. Sixteen-year-old Tommy Murphy... the *Boy Wonder*. People talk about David Clifford as a prodigy; anyone who saw young Tommy Murphy play would have smiled. He was that good, and he proved it with a goal that left even the Kerry supporters awe-struck. He went off injured though. Tim Landers got the crucial goal.

The final was even more sensational.

Kerry opened with two goals but were down one in the closing minutes. They got it to level but Cavan's Packie Boylan punched the ball over the bar just before the final whistle. Cavan erupted in ecstasy... then anger, as it turned out that the winning point was disallowed for a throw.

Match commentator Canon Michael Hamilton of Clare had already informed the nation that Cavan had won. Instead, it went to a replay, and Kerry won. It was the 'Landers Limited' final, the three brothers known as Lang, Purty, and Roundy (John Joe, Bill, and Tim) from Rock St all played for Kerry.

Dingle were the kingpins of the Kingdom by now, and the likes of Paddy Bawn Brosnan, Seán Brosnan, Bill Dillon and Bill Casey played crucial roles in winning Sam Maguire in 1940, '41 and '42. People were saying that Paddy Kennedy was even better than Pat 'Aeroplane' O'Shea or Larry Stanley as a fielder of a ball.

Five Kerry players featured in the 1942 All Ireland, but it was thin comfort to us; Dublin beat Galway. Work took players to many outposts and, travel being what it was, you made your bed where you made your living when it came to football.

The 1946 championship was delayed for the harvest – that was the hardest winter in living memory. The delay worked in Kerry's favour, as the county claimed its 16th title. Roscommon were cruising in the final, two goals clear and having hit the woodwork three times. Paddy Burke pulled back a goal. Roscommon captain Jimmy Murray was getting cleaned up after injury when Paddy Kennedy floated in a centre and big Tom O'Connor, nicknamed 'Gega' because of his size in primary school, rose high with his fist... poor Jimmy Murray's chance was gone for that year; Paddy and Gega goaled again in the replay.

The Polo Grounds in 1947.... *ouch!*

That's one of the most famous stories of them all, but in Kerry, it doesn't have a happy ending. Canon Michael Hamilton convinced Congress to play the final in New York as part of the centenary of the Great Famine that caused so many Irish people to go there. Kerry and Cavan made their way to New York, a huge adventure.

Kerry started well, but heat and injuries took their toll and Cavan emerged victorious. Plenty of Kerry supporters felt that it might have been different if Dr Eamonn had been there to train Kerry, but he wasn't invited by the county board. Mere trainers had no influence or power, even in team selection, but Dr Eamonn deserved better.

The Polo Grounds in Manhattan was a famous baseball and American Football ground, but it went the way of progress in 1964.

That defeat seemed to take it out of Kerry. Cavan and Mayo shared two titles each, with Meath winning and losing one over the following five years. Kerry were in what's now called a 'period of transition', which is a complicated way of saying 'not quite good enough'.

DONIE KNEW OF many of these stories as he was growing up.

He would have been running around and playing with the other children while adults gathered to listen on the radio and agree (or, human nature being what it is, disagree) with Michael O'Hehir.

He would have known exactly who every Kerry footballer was in terms of prowess and stature and skill, but he probably wouldn't have recognised any of them face to face.

The 50s were very hard times generally (Cahirsiveen native John Murphy's construction company in England employed more Irishmen than anyone in Ireland and more than anyone in England, except the Robert McAlpine builders, who became known as 'McAlpine's Fusiliers'). Three All-Ireland titles and runners-up once.

In 1953, the day that two gates broke down (thousands entered for free – it may have had the highest attendance of any All-Ireland final, but we'll never know) Kerry faced Armagh. No team from the Six Counties had ever won the All-Ireland. Cavan, the 1952 champions, had all of Ulster's four titles to date.

Armagh got an early goal. Tadhgie Lyne, the man they called the 'Prince of Forwards', was living up to his reputation as a distance kicker and edged Kerry into the lead. Then Johnny Foley handled the ball on the goal-line (illegal for goalkeepers back then) and Armagh had a penalty to go back in front. The penalty miss by Bill McCorry was still a subject of conversation at his funeral many years later.

In 1954, Kerry were made to work hard to beat Cork in Munster and then Galway in the semi-final. Meath were our All-Ireland final opponents and not fancied – they had only beaten Wicklow in the 'Long Count' Leinter final (nine minutes of injury time would raise eyebrows even nowadays; back then it was astonishing). Meath had the three best footballers on the pitch – Paddy O'Brien at full-back, Michael Grace as Man of the Match around the middle, and Peter McDermott, the famous 'Man in the Cap' up front.

As he lifted the cup, McDermott said that, 'beating Kerry is worth two All-Irelands'. We can be sore losers at times but McDermott made no enemies that day.

One of the great finals was right around the corner.

Dublin had been an early power in the GAA but had pretty much faded away. Part of that was simply that soccer had far more of a grip in the capital than anywhere else. In cosmopolitan Dublin, the 50s would literally see thousands flocking to see the likes of the great Shamrock Rovers teams of that era, while people thrilled to hear of the likes of Con Martin, Paddy Coad and Johnny Carey across the water.

Gaelic football?

It belonged mainly to those who moved to work and live in the city... gardai and teachers and the likes. The Dubs were literally and metaphorically blue collar. There had been great Dublin teams of the past, but they weren't Dubliners.

Until the 1950s.

Until St Vincent's in particular.

IT WOULD BE wrong to say that we ever feared Dublin, and an enormous insult to suggest that there was ever hatred there on either side, but there certainly was an antipathy born of respect.

In 1955, Dublin people were getting behind a fast, clever, brave team of Dubliners who were more than willing to go toe-to-toe with anyone, especially Kerry. Thirteen of the starting team were Vincents' players. Johnny Boyle and Jim McGuinness were the exceptions. Roving full-forward Kevin Heffernan was key to their play, having already roasted none other than the great O'Brien in Leinster.

Kerry's Dr Eamonn O'Sullivan had always lived by the football mantra of staying in your own position and winning your own duel. Dublin trainer (there was no such thing as a 'manager' in those days – Heffernan would lead that revolution in time as well) Peter O'Reilly and Co. were more interested in winning the game than any personal duels.

The 1955 All-Ireland final was billed as a clash of styles – traditional versus modern… flair and innovation against time-woven tradition.

Hubris was leaning towards Dublin.

Only it wasn't.

Heffernan, carrying a slight knock, couldn't rove too far away from big and uncompromising Ned Roche, who was beating him fair and square to the ball. Seán Murphy had Padraig 'Jock' Haughey in his pocket. Strand Road maestro John Dowling won midfield, with McGuinness hobbling off with injury.

Tadhgie Lyne had Kerry well in front before Ollie Freaney got a goal to make the finish tense. When the final whistle sounded, Kerry were still the undisputable masters of the game. It was an iconic moment, and Heffernan for one would carry the hard lessons of it forward.

Watching, on his first visit to Croke Park, Donie would also 'live' the game for some time.

Two titles and some close-run things (and a loss to Waterford in the first round in 1957…. news that hit the county like a tidal wave). A decent decade by Kerry standards, but not exceptional (which tells you everything you could ever need to know about our unrealistic standards). Mick O'Connell was captain as Kerry faced Galway in the final in 1959. Two goals from Dan McAuliffe and another from Garry McMahon saw Kerry take the title, and O'Connell, famously, left the Sam Maguire in the dressing-room. It adds hugely to his popular mystique.

O'Connell wasn't being disrespectful or dismissive about anything – that's simply not and never has been in his nature. There's no arrogance in O'Connell, never was. He was a brilliant footballer, but it was a craft he honed carefully. He was minding an injury, and simply assumed that a county board official would be taking charge of the cup.

THE 1960s WOULD bring more heartbreak than glory in Kerry's direction.

Three titles in the 1950s kept folk happy enough, but the decade that followed would see the Sam Maguire Cup journey down just twice. The 60s would also see

Kerry lose four All-Ireland finals, twice to Down in 1960 and '68 and, in between, twice in successive years to Galway.

The Tribesmen had five points to the good in 1964, and three in '65. Not learning from defeat to an enemy hurts, and it hurts even more when those defeats follow hot on one another's heels.

Two-thirds of Donie O'Sullivan's life as a Kerry footballer would be spread out across the fairly torturous 60s, when Down and Galway shared top-billing.

'It was a tough decade!' Donie admits.

'Looking back, we appreciate it even more how good that Down team was. They broke through from their own province and it was so important that they did, for their own county, but also for the game of football.

'They had to come through Cavan, Armagh, Donegal and Derry, and they did... Down had great players and very good systems of playing.

'They were a very strong team, and above all they had excellent forwards. Then Galway took over after them for their three years. It was hard on Kerry supporters, but in hindsight, looking back, you realise that it is also good to experience defeat sometimes in life.

'Life is full of knocks, and football can help you to prepare for the real knocks in life. Later, when our youngest son, Eoin got very sick... I found it hard to handle it. Áine was much better than me in dealing with his illness.

'Dr Joe Arthurs, he was our doctor... one day he asked me, "How many matches have you played for Kerry? How many championships... and you won and you lost, didn't you? You had the courage and the strength to keep going after those games, and you will have the same courage and strength here."

'And we did find the strength together. Going up to Dublin, to Crumlin Children's Hospital with Eoin... and then going up again the following month, we found our strength...'

The majesty of Fitzgerald Stadium Killarney. And Michael O'Hehir, the voice of the GAA when Donie was a young man, at work in Croke Park.

« CHAPTER 5 »

BY THE CUSP of 1960, Kerry looked, unquestionably, lords and masters of all they surveyed. Very few people in Kerry or anywhere else could have predicted the team that would dethrone us. And all of those few people would have been in an under-rated county that would become one of the greatest teams of all.

Hindsight, that canniest and most useless of generals, makes the threat of Down obvious. They had first cousins Seán (star of the 1958 minor final) and Kevin O'Neill, and James and Dan McCartan. Paddy Doherty was simply and clinically lethal in front of goal. Between February and November 1960, Doherty would clock up an incredible 11-77 in competitive matches for Down.

More than anything else, they had Maurice Hayes.

Hayes was the county secretary, but he was more like an eminence without the grise. By 1950 he was county secretary and he had long term plans for Down football. He, and county chairman Paddy O'Donoghue, were strongly in favour of a new and simplified team management. They got their man in 1958 with Barney Carr, with Maurice as one of his two selectors.

Before the All-Ireland final in 1960, Down brought in Peter McDermott to help them prepare for Kerry. Down had all their homework done and a completely new style of playing. In the finish, they were worthy All-Ireland champions. Kevin Mussen, team captain, would be the first man to bring the Sam Maguire Cup across the border. It wasn't only Kerry who felt that world had just tilted on its axis.

There was never any animosity between the players on either side. In fact, they got on quite well, and several of the Down team that were celebrating their historic win travelled down to Listowel for the races and met up with Kerry for a meal. The Kerry public were not so much rancourous, as simply shocked.

And it would get worse before it got better.

A year later Kerry reached the latter stages of the All-Ireland again and looked primed to correct that record. They blew everyone away in eight National League games (scoring a whopping 28 goals along the way) and crushing Cork in a replayed Munster final after they had the temerity to draw with Kerry in the first outing. That put them into a semi-final against Down.

John Dowling carried a knock into the game that hampered his mobility, but those were only excuses in hindsight. Down showed once and for all that they were reigning champions on merit alone and put Kerry right back into their box. Seán O'Neill got an early goal, though Kerry dominated late on… five '50s' in-a-row were cleared, and Down won by 1-12 to 0-9. They beat Offaly in the final.

Kerry needed new blood.

Good young footballers were coming through. A lot of eyes were on John Mitchels, who were heading for their third county title in-a-row at that stage and would end up with five, a record that still stands in Kerry.

But by that time Dr Crokes had a young footballer in midfield who was beginning to make a name for himself, even if he missed a lot of games because of his commitment to his Maynooth studies.

His name was Donie O'Sullivan.

WHILE DONIE WAS finishing his time in the Sem, Spa were beginning to struggle for numbers – an inevitable consequence in the economic decline and subsequent reliance on emigration. The club won three East Kerry junior titles in-a-row between 1957 and '59, but were struggling badly to field a senior team. Donie, who had always had the grá and actually had more skill than was immediately apparent (he lacked the commensurate strength to use it effectively) wanted to continue playing football.

A lot of the remaining Spa players, unable to field a team of their own, threw their lot in with St Finan's. The Kerry Mental Hospital was a huge employer in those times, and had some great footballers in their day. After all, the greatest football trainer of the age – and possibly any other – Dr Eamonn was the Resident Medical Supervisor who ran the place. St Finan's had some great players on their staff. Killarney Mental Hospital changed its name in 1959 to St Finan's, in honour of the hospital for lepers that had been founded in 869 AD by St Finan on Innisfallen.

The problem was that Donie was just a minor and not employed by the hospital in any way. St Finan's wasn't an option for him.

Most footballers from Spa had an affinity with Killarney Legion. In the 1930s, a common republican tradition and a certain rural kinship saw Spa players, like Jimmy and Paddy Fleming, Tadhg and Mick O'Sullivan, Paul Morris, Davy Fleming, Mick and Donie O'Leary, the Casey and Cahill brothers, and Jimmy Culloty don the Legion colours of green and white.

The famous story goes that James 'Micksie' Palmer, the former Cork minor and Kerry corner-back, had arranged to join Dr Crokes on his transfer to Killarney. When he alighted from the train near the Great Southern Hotel (now The Malton), a couple of people met him and brought him up to training and gave him a club jersey... green and white! Palmer had joined Legion, and would actually win a county championship with them in 1945.

Killarney Legion would be a natural fit for young Donie O'Sullivan from Tiernaboul. But Donie joined Dr Crokes instead. One could surmise, reasonably enough, that the great Jackie Looney (now Dr Crokes president, having won no less than 10 East Kerry titles) played a part. Or the fact that Fr Seán was a staunch Crokes' man.

There could be any number of reasons why Donie opted to join Dr Crokes. The real answer, though, is very simple pragmatism.

Donie smiles. 'Legion had a very strong minor team at the time,' he explains matter-of-factly. 'I wanted to play football.

'And I didn't believe I'd get on that team.'

THE INTRODUCTION OF a back door in a championship generated a lot of debate before the All-Ireland Championship in 2002. What wasn't mentioned much was that it wasn't a new idea by any means. County championships had taken many different forms over the years and a back door certainly wasn't a new concept.

Donie got a taste of it in his very first year playing senior for Dr Crokes. A year later, Donie was an automatic starter for the senior team, when he was available. That was an issue. A Maynooth student was very rigidly bound to the college's tight schedule.

There was no question of any leeway in that.

When Donie was free to play, he always played for Crokes, and never had any qualms about the distance to travel or, for that matter, the significance of the game. But he, Fr Paddy O'Donoghue, and Jimmy Hegarty were frequent absentees from championship games – and all three were key players.

Crokes came up against John Mitchels in the preliminary round of the 1959 Kerry Senior Championship. And that was some Mitchels' team. Garry O'Mahony in goal. The four Sheehy brothers, the sons of John Joe. The O'Shea brothers, Derry and John 'Thorny', who honed their skills on the basketball court and excelled at both codes. Alan Conway in defence – Donie and himself would both be called in to the Kerry panel at the same time, but that was a long way off yet. Teddy O'Dowd – Timmy would become a favourite of Kerry supporters in the far-off 80s. Fred Lynch and Seamus Roche. Every one of them wore the Kerry geansaí at some point or other.

That Mitchels' team was a bit better at football than everybody else – and there were great teams around. As for trying to rough them out of it... well, a team might try that, but they would only try it once!

Coming up against Mitchels in the preliminary round wasn't good news. They weren't the force they would become, not quite, but they were well on the way. Mind you, Mitchels wouldn't exactly have been cheering with gusto at the news that they were meeting the Killarney outfit either.

Mitchels prevailed after a good game by 1-10 to 1-7 to consign Crokes to a back door. They were able to steady the ship there and see off Kerins O'Rahillys by 1-7 to 0-7.

The quarter-final saw them draw with Feale Rangers and face them in a replay in Ballylongford. It was an absolute cracker, but a missed penalty meant that Crokes lost out by two points and saw their dreams ended yet again.

Mitchels went on to win the county title on June 25, 1960, a final replay having been long delayed since the previous November.

Just one week later they faced Feale Rangers in the opening round of the 1960 Championship -and were walloped by 3-11 to 3-1. No one could have guessed that they wouldn't lose another county championship game until July 26, 1964.

No team in Kerry has ever matched that record – a Dr Crokes side that included the likes of Colm Cooper, Kieran O'Leary, Eoin Brosnan, Johnny Buckley, and Fionn Fitzgerald were going for five titles in-a-row in 2014 but were stymied by arch-rivals Killarney Legion in the third round.

Along that sweep of history, Mitchels also purchased their club grounds, George Nagle's pitch in Boherbee, from the Kerry County Board (who had originally purchased it with the aim of expanding Austin Stack Park right beside it, but simply didn't have the funds).

IN 1960 DR CROKES had a very good side – Jackie Looney, Con Clifford, the O'Shea brothers, Paddy 'Bomber' and Murt, Donal 'Socky' Lynch, and of course Tadhgie Lyne. Donie O'Sullivan was a good fit in that company, and this year he really stood out.

They dismissed St Brendan's with ease in the preliminary round. They beat Mid Kerry by double scores, 2-12 to 1-6, with Paddy 'Doc' O'Donoghue (brother of Mickey Doc, whose Park Place Hotel at the top of High St in Killarney was an unofficial headquarters of the Kerry team for many years) responsible for both goals.

The Kerryman newspaper noted that one 'Donal O'Sullivan' in midfield had played well. It was his first mention in the newspaper for football; they would get to know his name well before much longer. But that was a Crokes' side that included their students. Without Donie, Jimmy Hegarty, or Fr Paddy, Crokes were a diminished side and *The Kerryman* preview noted that *Donie O'Sullivan will be a huge loss* as they headed off to face champions John Mitchels.

The prediction was proven correct as Mitchels, at the peak of their formidable powers, blew them away. They scored four goals and it could have been more.

To suggest that no one had heard of Donie before this would be completely wrong. An up-and-coming midfielder for a senior club like Dr Crokes?

Of course, people knew him; they just hadn't known that he could do something like this.

Practically every child in Kerry grows up dreaming of wearing the green and gold. For Donie, the dream was fast becoming a reality.

The 1960s were quickly in the grasp of Paddy Doherty and the Down team (here Doherty leads his team in Croke Park in 1961).

Donie defending against Galway in the 1965 All-Ireland final, when the Connacht champs won their second of a three in-a-row of titles.

Mick O'Connell fields highest against Down in the 1968 All-Ireland final (but the northerners continued their dominance of the Kerrymen).

« CHAPTER 6 »

I DON'T KNOW when Kerry first adopted green and gold as their colours. In 1905 (the 1903 championship – delays were common in a time when infrastructure nationally, let alone in GAA, was in its infancy), Kerry lined out in the colours of county champions John Mitchels, green with a red trim. I have heard references subsequently to Kerry supporters wearing green and gold rosettes (the idea of hats, flags, scarves, or – and one can only shudder at the thought in those far off days – headbands, was preposterous) at matches in the early days, but none are convincing.

One story I have heard is that an early Kerry team set off to play a challenge game in Waterford, but forgot their jerseys. Kerry full-back Roderick 'Rody' Kirwan, was a bank official in Castleisland but was originally from Kilrosanty in Waterford and had represented his native county and Wexford before moving to Kerry. The Kirwans were all great athletes – Percy was possibly the best Irish athlete of his time as well as a dual Waterford player.

Kerry had forgotten their jerseys. Rody borrowed the green and gold jerseys of his old club instead. Kerry played well in them and won by a good margin and decided to stick to the colours. It's a lovely story, but how much of it is history and how much of it is myth is open to question.

Cork originally wore blue and yellow, but switched to red and white after the British Army stole their jerseys from Cook St (Cork GAA HQ at the time) and they had to borrow jerseys from Fr O'Leary's Total Abstinence Hall nearby. They have worn red and white ever since. Famously, when there was a clash of colours with Meath in the 1939 All-Ireland final, it was agreed that Kerry would line out in the red and white of county champions Dingle.

Unknown to many at the time, Jimmy McKenna of the Dingle Drapery family had served his apprenticeship with the famous Cork drapery business of Queen's Old Castle. While there, he had handled an order of county jerseys for the Cork County Board that were rejected. When Dingle were looking for a set of club jerseys for the 1938 county championship, club stalwart and trustee Jimmy brokered a deal with his old employers for the jerseys that had been rejected by the Cork County Board. Kerry duly won the All Ireland wearing them!

WHEN THE GAA decided that each county would nominate its chosen team colours in 1923, it was the legendary Pat 'Aeroplane' O'Shea of Castlegregory, one of the greatest midfielders ever to play for Kerry, who suggested green and gold, and it was unanimously agreed.

Every player in Kerry wanted to wear green and gold.

Donie was no exception, and his progress with Dr Crokes had put him very firmly on the radar, especially in the 1960 county championship. The grassroots in Kerry were hearing his name more and more often, and enquiries were being made on the quiet. He made the Kerry junior panel for the 1960 championship, the same year that the Liebherr factory formally opened in Killarney (building had commenced in 1958). That was a huge boost to the town – they have been big employers ever since and also own several local hotels.

That junior team was a very good side – Alan Conway (Mitchels) at full-back, Tomo Burke (Desmonds), Bernard O'Callaghan, Patrick 'Pop' Fitzgerald (Rahillys), Teddy O'Sullivan (Killarney Legion), Pat Aherne (Ballymacelligott), John McCarthy (Ballylongford)… all known and rated footballers.

All of them ranked above the quiet, young Crokes lad who wore No. 21 and never got a game as the team made it to the All-Ireland semi-final, only to bow out to Dublin.

Arrah… it was only a half-chance at best.

The Kerry juniors (which was the county's 'second' team in those days) have always been put well in the shade by the focus on the senior team. In fact, over the years, some players might be reluctant to play for the Kerry juniors because the quality of the football was so under-estimated. If you weren't absolutely spectacular at the lower grade, how could you be worth a look at the higher one?

The notion seems to be that Kerry footballers are born from the cradle rather than encouraged and developed – logic and reason are not always easy bedfellows.

Be that as it may, Donie was on the radar, but not exactly making any shockwaves as yet.

Donie was filling out, though. His frame was growing big enough to carry muscle, and no farmer's son had any problem developing muscle. Donie was no longer a stripling and well able to stand his ground against grown men now. After his impressive displays for Crokes in the past two years, the junior selectors decided to take a second look and Donie started against Cork in the Munster final on July 2, 1961. It was his first appearance in the Kerry jersey.

Interestingly, although Donie was best known at that stage as a midfielder, he played half-back. Kerry won by 2-4 to 0-6, and the new defender was one of those whose display was marked.

They lost out to eventual champions Louth in the All-Ireland semi-final. That was a great Louth team in its own right, with the likes of Gussie Sheehan, Paddy Jordan and Michael 'Muckle' McKeown on board, and they beat Meath, Offaly, Longford, Dublin, Kerry, Galway (in the 'Home' final) and Yorkshire to take the title.

'Losing that game to Louth was most disappointing,' says Donie. 'Louth got a last minute goal to win by a point. The final had been fixed for Croke Park for the following Sunday.

'At the time, I considered the final to be my one and only chance to play in Croke Park.'

Donie had worn a Kerry jersey, and worn it with distinction – but he had no medals to show for it yet. The names of many of his teammates have faded into history now...

Kerry: Tony Guerin (Emmett's); Denny Falvey (Annascaul), Alan Conway (John Mitchels), John Dalton (John Mitchels); Fred Lynch (John Mitchels), Con Clifford (Dr Crokes), Pa Kerins (Kerins O'Rahillys); Jerry O'Riordan (Glenbeigh), Donie O'Sullivan (Dr Crokes); R Broderick (Austin Stacks), Bobby Buckley (Ballyheigue), Paddy Hussey (Dingle); Weeshie Fogarty (Legion),

Joe Sheehy (Moyvane), Pat Ahern (Ballymac). Subs: Liam Dennehy (Kerins O'Rahillys), Paddy Purtill (Ballylongford), Tim Gunn (Ballydonoghue), Louis Nolan (Legion), Liam Chute (Ballymac).

THOSE TWO DEFEATS to Down were still stinging Kerry supporters and they needed a good start to 1962, if the grumbles weren't to get a lot louder. The National League didn't go as Kerry planned and didn't engender confidence. They lost to Carlow in Tralee in their opening match, beat Kildare by 0-12 to 0-6, hammered Wexford (Dan McAuliffe of Duagh had 1-6 and John Burke from Milltown scored two goals) before going down to Cork by a point. They beat Offaly in the Wembley Tournament to calm the nerves – only to be walloped by Roscommon in Killarney. That put the cat right in among the pigeons and sharpening its claws in Kerry!

Kerry were trying to find defenders, with the likes of Louis Nolan, Alan Conway and Seán Óg Sheehy tried in the backs – even Tom Long, who had always played in midfield or in the forwards, was transported back to centre-back. Nothing was quite clicking.

John Dowling and Jackie Lyne, two of Kerry's greatest players, had stepped down as selectors but of the five-man selection committee (elected at convention in January, as was customary until the late 90s in Kerry) only Fr Denis Curtin hadn't won an All-Ireland on the field of play – and he was as good a judge as any of them. Johnny Walsh of Ballylongford, John Joe Sheehy of Mitchels, Paddy Bawn Brosnan of Dingle, Murt Kelly of Beaufort – these were known men.

The trainer of the Kerry team was Dr Eamonn O'Sullivan, who had just been elected president of Kerry GAA as well after retiring from his post in St Finan's Hospital.

Dr Eamonn had led Kerry to All-Irelands in 1924, '26, '37, '46, and '53. No one had any issues with the personnel on the sideline… but there were real doubts about some of the players on the other side of the same line.

There were five debutants in Frank Sheehy Park in Listowel for the Munster semi-final victory over Waterford, but Donie wasn't one of them. There were two more changes for the provincial final against Cork, which Kerry would win handsomely, 4-8 to 0-4, at their opponents' Athletic Grounds (revamped and re-named Pairc Uí Caoimh in 1976).

Gene O'Driscoll of Annascaul came in at centre-forward and Donie O'Sullivan replaced Alan Conway at right full-back. Donie had no name as a corner-back, not yet – he played in the engine room of midfield or centre-back on all his club teams. Even then, though, the power of his long-distance kick was a potent weapon, and it's not unreasonable to guess that it was one motive for his selection. Keepers didn't take the kick-outs in those days, and as for short kick-outs – they did occasionally happen, but they were very much looked on as a necessary evil.

Mick O'Connell and Jimmy Lucey in midfield?

Sure, why wouldn't you be belting the ball out to that pair of fielders? Donie wasn't nervous. A championship debut is a huge step for any player, but Donie knew the quality of the men around him.

'For all of us who were young playing then, you had a strong nucleus. A very strong, experienced group of players from Johnny Culloty in goals... Niall Sheehy, Tim Lyons, Seamus Murphy, Mick O'Dwyer, Tom Long, Mick O'Connell, Dan McAuliffe. That was half a team already in itself.

'I was very inexperienced in 1962. I felt I was put in there at corner-back to kick out the ball and I remember at one stage, after being hit fairly, looking up at the sky, thinking... *I shouldn't be here at all, I'm not fit for this.*

'But Dr Eamonn, and that's what we called him... Dr Eamonn, he wasn't like a formal manager of today. We had huge respect for him and all that he had done, but he would always be encouraging... and he was always pleasant. He looked out for us, and he'd sit down and have a chat with a player. It was very personal.'

Donie had been down to mark Joe O'Sullivan of Castletownbere but O'Sullivan was switched to centre-forward on Noel Lucey instead, and Noel was sent off in the second-half. That was far from the only flare-up in the game. The atmosphere on the field was tense and physical, with scores real and imagined being settled, as a follow on from the National League earlier in the year. Moss Colbert from Limerick was a very good referee, but no referee could have reined this in. The old Athletic Field was packed, and the atmosphere electric.

'It was a real baptism of fire,' recalls Donie.

Kerry took command. 'Tom Long was one of the greatest footballers and he showed it that afternoon. He was also, more importantly, a wonderful person and a loyal friend.' It was Long who set up Dan McAuliffe early on for a goal and added another himself straight after. Gene O'Driscoll fisted home a third goal from a Paudie Sheehy free and Kerry were ahead by 3-4 to 0-2 at half-time.

The contest was well over by the time Mick O'Connell scored Kerry's fourth goal. But by then, Cork's Eric Ryan, a fantastic player and huge crowd favourite, had to be carried off injured and that saw furious supporters pelt Johnny Culloty's goal with sods and stones (the terraces weren't concreted).

The umpires had to shelter inside the net with Johnny.

Con Paddy O'Sullivan from Urhan was midfield for Cork. It was Donie's first encounter with someone who would also soon become a lifelong and valued friend.

'Con has been like an angel of mercy. He lives near the Cork University hospital there and we'd often call in to him when visiting there; Con was great to us, as were Gene McCarthy and Johnny Carroll too… I know them well, we'd often still meet. And the same with Kevin Dillon down in Clonakilty. Pat Griffin died recently and when we'd call down to him, Kevin was so good to all of us."

As debuts go, it was as comfortable as it could get score-wise, and the exact opposite in terms of football. In the circumstances, it's worth remembering the first Kerry senior team that Donie played with. It might have been a baptism of fire in some ways, but he had strong men beside him.

Kerry: Johnny Culloty; Donie O'Sullivan, Niall Sheehy, Tim 'Tiger' Lyons; Seamus Murphy, Noel Lucey, Mick O'Dwyer; Mick O'Connell, Jimmy Lucey; Dave Geaney, Gene O'Driscoll, Seán Óg Sheehy; Dan McAuliffe, Tom Long, Paudie Sheehy.

ON JULY 29, CAVAN faced Down in Casement Park for the Ulster final. Down, twice reigning All-Ireland champions, were expected to see off Cavan comfortably.

Cavan had once been the undisputed kingpins of Ulster, but those days were in the past. In 1960, *Gaelic Weekly* magazine had written to Cavan to uninvite them to the annual tournament sponsored by the paper – Cavan simply weren't worth watching. That one stung, but Cavan stayed quiet.

Down had been completely understrength in Cavan's National League win; nobody was reading too much into that one. By the time the championship came around, Cavan were filling their ranks with lads from their successful junior team, including schoolboys Ray Carolan and Jimmy Stafford. What people didn't realise was that these weren't ordinary schoolboys.

They had won back-to-back McRory Cups with St Pat's of Cavan and, with the joyous inhibition and certainty of youth, were under-awed by Down's reputation. It rapidly showed on the day as Cavan took control right from the start. Carolan lorded midfield, Jimmy Stafford struck for two goals and set up James Brady for another.

Charlie Gallagher was at his spectacular best. In the end, it was 3-6 to 0-5 to the underdogs. That was a huge fillip for Cavan football.

It was also a huge boost to the watching Kerrymen, and they knew it. With Down gone, the whole championship was blown wide open. There is a certain similarity to sharks with elite sportsmen – they could all smell blood in the water now.

RTÉ HAD STARTED broadcasting on New Year's Eve 1961. By 1962, TV programmes such as *Radharc* and Paddy Crosbie's *The School Around the Corner* were becoming hugely popular. Charles Mitchell was RTÉ's first news broadcaster, and one of the news events that the new station covered superbly was the visit of Princess Grace and Prince Rainier to Ireland. Cassius Clay – yet to fight Sonny Liston and change his name to Muhammad Ali – and The Beatles (controversially – the gardaí were completely unprepared for the crowds of teenagers) would follow in the same year.

John F Kennedy, the Irish-American Catholic President of the United States, was a powerful symbol of an age of hope and Irish confidence, and he too visited. A few short months after riding through Dublin in an open limousine, he was shot dead in Dallas – certain American aspirations seemed to die that day as well. For years afterwards Irish culture could be summed up by three pictures that graced the walls of so many houses it became a cliché founded on truth – JFK, the Pope, and De Valera.

By 1962, Teilifís Eireann was ready for its first outside sports broadcast, and the All-Ireland semi-final between Kerry and Dublin was an obvious choice.

Dublin were not the power they would become in the 1970s, but Dublin and Kerry had a cachet all of its own, even then. Dublin, after all, had been the champions in 1959. They were always there or thereabouts. Soccer was still the bigger game in the city, but a Dublin-centric media reckoned that Dublin had a great chance. In fairness, the national media have always tended to shine a constant spotlight on Dublin (the biggest population is obviously their largest market) even in the capital's harder days, and it never really helped Dublin's cause. Mind you, they had some real quality players in 1962… the likes of the Foley brothers, John Timmons, Dessie Ferguson, Cathal O'Leary, Paddy Holden, Heffernan and Mickey Whelan.

The idea of TV coverage being available was not universally popular, with a lot of officials worried that match attendances would be affected. Their fears were confirmed when just over 60,000 made their way to Croke Park, a drop of over 11,000 on the 1961 attendance. In fact, the coverage was top quality, with Teilifís Eireann doing a great job.

Dr Eamonn had his ways with a team before a game of this importance, and he had his *ways* with each individual too.

'He would have a good talk with us on the Thursday night before the match and he would go through the team. Before the game against Dublin, he began… "Johnny Culloty"… but then he went to the opposite corner of the full-back line, he went… "Tim Lyons, Niall Sheehy…" and then he came to me. He had a word for every player about what he wanted of them.

'I was so green… the innocence, but when Dr Eamonn came to me and said my name, he then went on… "I have nothing at all to say to you, just go out and play your own game… you'll have no problems!" He said this in front of everybody. I thought to myself… *What is he thinking? What's wrong with this man?*

'It was years later that it dawned on me what he had been at. This was Dr Eamonn with a young footballer, telling the young footballer not to be worried, not to think too much about what he needed to do.

'He knew also that I was not out there on my own on the field… there were other men to talk to me out there too… Johnny Culloty, Niall Sheehy and Tim Lyons and the other lads.

'They would also be gentle and encouraging to me.

'The Saturday evening before the game, in Bray, he gave us all a little card and printed on the card were four points… 'Fear. Fatal. Fouling'… and the fourth one was to conserve your energy. He believed in people, and he also had a very strong religious faith. He'd have the rosary in the evening… he'd never push it, but the whole team would take part.'

The hand of Dr Eamonn O'Sullivan, however, was always on a young Donie O'Sullivan in his formative years as a Kerry footballer. Donie casts his mind back to a game in Longford, before 1962, a tournament game, but a game for an inexperienced Donie which was simply huge in his own mind.

'I wasn't on the championship team at the time, and I didn't really know what was happening. Dr Eamonn was working and we had to wait for him for half an hour, maybe an hour, and it was very late when we all got into Longford. Everywhere was closed.

'He had thought we might be able to get a cup of team and a sandwich or something when we got there, but we had nothing. We all went to our rooms, where we were staying.

'About 10 minutes later, there was a knock on my door. It was Dr Eamonn, and he walked into my room, and he had a glass of milk and some biscuits for me. He had gone to that trouble, just to make sure that I got something to eat.'

Donie was attending St John's University in the US, and was unable to attend Dr Eamonn's funeral when he died just a few years later, in 1966.

He remembers, still, a man whom some who did not know him thought of as remote, but someone whom the Kerry footballers knew as a big family man, with a big heart, and a love for every Kerry team he touched. 'We had the highest respect for him!' states Donie. 'The things he did for us all, the way he prepared us... the way he convinced us to believe in ourselves.'

KERRY, EVEN WITHOUT the suspended Noel Lucey, looked more assured than they had been all year. Dublin, on the other hand, were slow to settle and paid a high price early on.

After five minutes, Donie's Dr Crokes teammate Tom Long caught a Paudie Sheehy free and fired it past Paschal Flynn into the net. Long and Sheehy combined again, setting up Garry McMahon for goal number two.

At half-time it was 2-9 to 0-3 and the game was over as a contest.

Dublin did rally, cutting the gap to seven points and hitting the crossbar, but Kerry were able to lift their game again and rattle off three points in a minute. Donie was one of the players singled out for particular praise in match reports afterwards, as were Mick O'Connell and Tom Long, of course; O'Connell scored from two sideline kicks during the game. He smiles with genuine amusement at the memory.

'There might have been a bit more to that than most of the spectators realised!' he laughs. 'I was on Kevin Heffernan, who was well established as one of Dublin's greatest ever footballers by then. Heffernan was Dublin to the core, one of the St Vincent's people who wanted Dubliners to represent the county at gaelic games… not lads from other counties working in Dublin, as had been the case more often than not before the 50s.'

In 1934, when Dublin beat Kerry in the All-Ireland semi-final in Tralee (it became known as 'Ham Sunday' because of the amount of sandwiches left over) it gave them a solid core of support in the city, something that hadn't previously been there.

In 1962, Dublin were getting beaten, and Heffernan never bowed down easily to any team. He was Dublin captain, and he had already decided that this would be his last year playing for the county. It was almost time, but he was determined to throw everything he had into these couple of games.

Heffernan had been on many beaten Dublin teams, but they didn't capitulate like this. Not even to Kerry. Not to anyone.

Donie, as he says himself, was 'lacking in experience and self-confidence'. His famous lengthy kick wasn't too much in evidence. In later years, he could read a game almost sub-consciously, but right now, at 22 years of age, he was relying on strength and speed and he had plenty of both. Johnny Culloty, Niall Sheehy, and Tim Lyons were the voices he heeded, and they didn't lead him astray.

Donie was as strong as Heffernan and that little bit faster. He was also a total footballer, with rare concentration. He eschewed the spectacular; he already knew that 'winning football' is 'team football' and he relentlessly gathered up ball and sent it back out to Kerrymen. Heffernan was getting frustrated, and his duel with Donie was becoming more robust and physical as time went on.

'Heffernan was a very good footballer, and physical and tough aswell," explains Donie. 'But football in Maynooth had also been very physical and we had a saying at the time… in Latin. "Ne Plus Ultra"… beyond which your opponent shall not go. That pertained to my experience in the 1962 All-Ireland semi-final.'

Eventually, Heffernan, not expecting a reprisal to one more tough and robust challenge, was flat on his back.

Donie, being *Donie*, was mortified.

He moved over to help the Dublin captain back to his feet.

Big Niall Sheehy, Kerry's tough-as-nails full back, moved to intercept. He caught Donie by the shoulder.

'Will you come on away now!' he beseeched the corner-back, 'And lave the crathur to die a natural death?'

'Heffernan was a great player!' Donie further explains. 'That day, I suppose, he thought I was green enough. He caught me with a dummy early on and he could have taken his point, but he was going for goal. I caught him on the second dummy.

'He lost the ball… and the ball went wide. I don't know if that upset him or not. There were no words, he never said a thing to me. I kicked the next ball and… next thing, it was like there was an explosion. I didn't know what had happened… I could barely see the people in the stand.

'It was a desperate feeling, because I could hear the shouting and roaring. I got back up onto my feet, and we played on. Before we came out for the second-half, I was given smelling salts… they nearly blew the head off me!

'I was really annoyed, and at the same time I hardly knew where I was or what was happening. Heffernan then went on a bit of a solo run and he let the ball go out in front of him, too far… and I pulled on it.

'That's when he went down.

'It was a battle alright, but I can't remember a lot of it. Most of the game was a blur to me after I got hit. At one stage I had no idea how much time was left, and I was placing the ball for a kick out.

'I could barely see the bloody ball I was supposed to be kicking. I was looking at it, but I couldn't see it. I shouldn't have been on the field.

'Johnny Culloty came up to me and he said, "Don't worry… we're in the All-Ireland final, just kick it!"'

Kevin Heffernan shook both their hands at the final whistle, as he and Donie departed the field with a mutual respect for one another, which would endure.

Heffernan always wanted to beat Kerry, but it was never personal. In a time where a lot of Dublin people scorned the 'culchie' sports, Heffernan, who had grown up in narrow streets that were just as much a breeding ground for tough footballers as the fields that Donie had played on in his younger days, had learned to see Kerry as the benchmark. Tough farmers and hardy fishermen. Heffernan learned every lesson and dished out a few along the way as well.

KERRY WERE BACK in the All-Ireland final, and meeting the team that had beaten them in 1944 and should have beaten them in '46 (Kerry won thanks to two late goals from Tom 'Gega' O'Connor and Paddy Kennedy).

Roscommon had emerged again from the West and brought hearts and minds with them. This was a more seasoned Kerry, though, who had been in the latter stages of the last four All-Ireland Championships.

Roscommon were not. They had been rather fortunate to win the Connacht final. Sligo had a string of late injuries and missed a '50' while two points clear before Roscommon, having trailed for most of the game, stuck a very late goal to win it.

In the All-Ireland semi-final, Cavan, having emerged from Ulster for their first time in seven years, weren't able to find their rhythm in Croke Park and didn't do themselves justice against Roscommon.

Kerry, then, had good reasons to be optimistic as they made their way to Croke Park for the final.

Well, most of them.

One player was noticeably absent.

Donie was back in Maynooth. He wouldn't even be attending the game as a spectator, having played and shone in every game right up to the final.

'I was in Maynooth at the time in the seminary, and we just didn't get out to play games. We could play during our holidays, but the college schedule was strictly adhered to, and that wasn't up for negotiation.

'Of course, it was a big game... and, of course, I would have loved to have played, but the rules were there. It had happened to John Kennedy of Galway in 1959. He was a great footballer, but he wasn't allowed out for the All-Ireland final... and Galway lost.

'At least Kerry won in 1962.

'That was it. Of course, it was disappointing, being young and seeing all the rest in Croke Park playing and winning and not being there.

'Nobody forced me to stay... the gates weren't locked.

'I thought about it and I decided fairly fast... that "no", I wasn't going to go and play. As well, it was of the times, and it was an accepted thing. Dr Eamonn and the others were so supportive, especially Jimmy Lucey.

'They probably talked about it amongst themselves, and might have wondered what I would do, but nobody would think of bringing it up in conversation once I had made my own decision. They accepted it.

'They were excellent that way... and not one player said anything to me, there was no pressure.'

Donie O'Sullivan watched the 1962 All-Ireland final on television in Maynooth College, with fellow students and an assortment of other people. 'I was prepared for it, and I had decided to live with my decision by the Sunday.

'That was it, in my mind.

'I did imagine myself sitting in the dressing-room... and running out onto the field with my teammates. But I had made my decision, nobody had forced me to miss the game. After I had made my decision, Dr Jim Brosnan had told me that I would still be named on the official panel, and that if Kerry won... I would have an All-Ireland medal.

'I was thankful for that, of course, very grateful, especially years later when I looked back on it all.'

IT WASN'T A new story for young clerics and clerical students.

Castleisland native Redmund Prendeville, known to all and sundry as 'Mundy', had been a clerical student in All Hallows, Dublin, back in 1924. Selected for Kerry at midfield in that year's All-Ireland final, the gravitational pull of the green and gold was a small bit stronger than the collar.

Mundy won his All-Ireland medal as Kerry beat Dublin by 0-4 to 0-3. Expelled from All Hallows, he was able to finish his studies and be ordained in St Kieran's College, Kilkenny. In 1935, he became the world's youngest Archbishop when he was appointed to the diocese of Perth in Australia.

He is said to have sent a letter to the president of All Hallows, Rev Thomas O'Donnell (the two men actually got on well and the president had been one of those who ensured that Mundy was able to qualify after his expulsion) citing the biblical quotation from the Psalms... *The stone once rejected by the builder has become the corner-stone.*

Rev O'Donnell, who had a keen sense of humour himself, replied drily, 'We never cease to wonder at the works of the Lord!'

Dr Jim Brosnan's Kerry minors won their final in 1962 – with Jimmy O'Mahoney scoring three goals – by a whopping 6-5 to 0-7, and goalkeeper

Seamus Mac Gearailt made his way to the senior sub's bench just in case Johnny Culloty picked up an injury during the game. At that time, senior teams only had a panel of 20 players and usually no sub keeper.

Donie was replaced at corner-back by Seamus Murphy, with Noel Lucey coming into the team at centre-back.

Garry McMahon's goal in the 1962 final is up there with the likes of Din Joe Crowley's in 1970, Seamus Darby's in 1982 or Kevin McManamon's in 2011.

Referee Eamon Moules of Wicklow threw in the ball and Roscommon attacked. Tim Tiger Lyons cut out the ball and passed to Timmy O'Sullivan on the Cusack side. Timmy was fouled and Mick O'Connell kicked the free high into his 1955 minor teammate Garry. Oliver Moran and John Lynch, two good defenders, both went to intercept it and accidentally blocked each other. Garry timed it perfectly and fisted the ball past goalkeeper Aidan Brady.

Garry himself said afterwards that Johnny Walsh had advised him that Roscommon's defenders tended to attack everything and could leave such an opening.

Kerry added five points on the trot, three of them from O'Connell, after 18 minutes. Roscommon did score a penalty but Kerry hit another three points to Roscommon's one just before half-time. Kerry were ahead by 1-8 to 1-1. Kerry only scored four points in the second-half, one of them a real beauty by O'Connell, but Roscommon only had five.

Donie, who may have missed that final but doesn't feel sorry for himself, has a lot of sympathy for that Roscommon side, and one player in particular whom he always admired.

'You don't blame Roscommon. They were trying to slow it down a bit. They didn't have all the luck, either, because apart from conceding the early goal, Gerry O'Malley got injured.

'He had to go off... centre-back... fabulous player... footballer and hurler. He never won an All-Ireland medal... he played for years and years.

'That was his final.

'He was captain. They lost and he got injured.'

THE YEAR THAT Donie's Kerry career took off in earnest was almost the year that the world ended. JFK in the US and Nikita Khrushchev in the Soviet

Union both had access to nuclear missiles, and Khrushchev wanted to put some in communist Cuba. The world was poised on the brink of nuclear war until the Soviets blinked at the last second, but it was a very close and very terrifying thing.

For the GAA the 'Ban' was again on the agenda. Ballylongford brought a motion to have it removed to the Kerry county convention. It was so vehemently opposed on the night that when it went to a vote, even the proposer and seconder voted against it.

Unbeknownst to Donie, a meeting in the old Macra na Feirme Hall in March would have a profound effect on his future. Spa didn't have the numbers for a senior team, but they weren't the kind of people to give up the ghost of a viable club in the area without at least throwing a bit of holy water at it. The club was reformed, at least at juvenile level.

Con Doherty was chairman, with Paddy Dennehy as secretary and Johnny Doolan as treasurer. Within a year they would amalgamate with Glenflesk (Spa and Glenflesk players had lined out together with Headford in the early days of Kerry football) to win the East Kerry Minor League. Maybe it would only be a futile gesture of defiance against fate.

Or maybe it would be a pebble that would start an avalanche that would change the local sporting landscape forever. Time would tell.

DR EAMONN O'SULLIVAN, as already stated, was the undisputed architect of Kerry success between 1925 and '65. He was the trainer ('management' was the sole preserve of county board officials).

It was still widely believed that the famous 1947 loss in New York's Polo Grounds would not have happened if Dr Eamonn had travelled with the team as manager – there has never been a convincing reason put forward for not selecting him. Dr Eamonn did not receive any renumeration for his work with the Kerry team (or seek any), nor was he allowed on any trips away with them.

In 1960, disappointed at the facilities provided for the Kerry players (not himself – he was a players' man always) he stepped down. Johnny Walsh of Shannon Rangers, who was arguably the heart and soul of North Kerry football for nigh on half a century, and Gerald O'Sullivan of Killarney Legion did the training instead.

Both were great footballers – Walsh was a selector and trainer of teams across all grades for Kerry for many years, while O'Sullivan had inspired South Kerry's first-ever county title win in 1955. But they weren't Dr Eamonn, and his absence was enough to cause serious tension within the camp, nearly a full-blown strike. Dr Eamonn was *primus* – anyone else, even greats like Walsh and O'Sullivan, were *pares*.

In the day, travel took much longer, even where it was available. It was impractical for players inside the county, let alone students or people working elsewhere. No, players were expected to maintain a good level of fitness themselves as well as practicing their kicking, especially on their weaker foot. Dr Eamonn was very much in favour of collective training camps prior to the bigger games. Players would stay together (almost always in Killarney) and followed a strict but not demanding routine.

They would sleep for at least seven hours.

They would arise at the scheduled time and do a group breathing and stretching session, and take a 15- to 20-minute walk.

Not a run or a jog… a clam, measured walk.

Breakfast would be porridge with a small fry (or fish and eggs on a Friday, of course, as Catholic tradition demanded) and tea and toast. Players would rest completely for a full hour in order to digest the food properly.

At 11am Dr Eamonn would give a structured lecture featuring no more than two aspects of play – he wanted the players to be aware of distinct points rather than swamped with detail.

Lectures were short (no more than 15 minutes), and clear. The importance of mental training was recognised by the highly respected psychiatrist.

As a defender, Donie would be one of many over generations who would quickly recognise one of Dr Eamonn's most important mantras… that of 'Fear. Fatal. Fouling'.

Stay tight… first to the ball… do not go off gallivanting elsewhere on the pitch. Read the situation, think on the field… and do not concede frees, make the opposing player work for the score. Dr Eamonn believed that any Kerry footballer was better one-on-one with any opponent and should actively take on such duels in the expectation of winning them.

If you were to mention the idea of a blanket defence in those days, you would be strongly advised to meet with Dr Eamonn O'Sullivan – in his professional capacity!

Players would then tog out and do an hour-long session. A 500 yards jog (not a full-on run; it was about warming up the muscles, not testing them) followed by physical drills and ball-work, usually focused on the tactics spoken of in his earlier lecture. Dr Eamonn was using plyometric training that included skipping ropes, players 'leap-frogging' each other, strength training where the focus was on repetition rather than weight, and core muscle work long before the term 'plyometric' was even invented!

That would be followed by lunch and an hour-long rest period for digestion. Lunch, not supper, was the main meal of the day. Though out-dated now, it had a strong resonance then.

Another short lecture would follow, and then a 90-minute session.

Dinner would be served at 6pm, a lighter meal. After the rest period, Dr Eamonn would have some form of relaxing entertainment arranged – walks, concerts, cinema visits, an amateur drama show. There would be a light supper of milk and biscuits. The stimulant tea was to be avoided at such a time – good sleep and regular rest were even more of a priority than the actual training sessions. Kerry won eight All-Ireland titles using these training methods.

It's not a coincidence. The idea of rest being as important as training... and warm-ups, core training, diet... these were so far ahead of their time. A lot of professional sports teams in Britain and the US were also far behind anything Dr Eamonn was doing.

Donie O'Sullivan (right), the Kerry captain, strolling in Killarney with Johnny Culloty, the 1969 team captain, and Jerry O'Leary who had seen every one of Kerry's 21 All-Ireland victories since 1903.

« CHAPTER 7 »

IT WAS A big year for Donie.

It was something that had been buzzing around in his mind for quite a while. Maynooth was a wonderfully enriching experience – but his feeling was that his future lay elsewhere. He wasn't cut out for the priesthood.

It was a momentous decision. It was a very dramatic change. Except that it was inevitable by then.

Maynooth had welcomed record numbers of students during the 1950s. Well-intentioned administrators saw new buildings to welcome the influx. Government grants and episcopal funding increased. But the old intellectual rigour of the courses had changed little over the decades, while the world outside was in a state of flux. 'We were continually questioning,' Donie recalls.

After much personal deliberation, Donie sought answers elsewhere.

'It's wasn't a decision that happened overnight, it went through my mind for many months,' he explains. 'You had to make up your own mind eventually.

'If you enjoyed sport, as I did, it would have been easy enough to stay and drift through it all, but it had come to a stage where a decision had to be made.

'I believed that I had reached that point.

'I left with no regrets, nor with anything but gratitude toward the many people who had helped me. There was certainly no weakening of faith in God, Christianity or the Church.

'There was no pressure from my family to stay, and I talked to Tim about it, of course, and he was very supportive.

'His standards were higher than mine.

'My mother certainly didn't worry about my leaving.

'Her sister, Mary, in America wrote to her and she told my mother that she was very happy I was leaving Maynooth and that… "One priest in the family is enough!" That was a sensible thing to say at the time, and a humorous comment which my mother appreciated.

'My father didn't say much to me at about it, that I can remember. He realised I was my own man at that stage, and had to make my own way through life. But, for me, it was still stressful, and it was still difficult coming out.

'Without the football, it would have been even more difficult.'

Donie began playing his football in Dublin. Not too long after he left – on January 25, 1963 – he remembers getting a bus into the city centre, and getting off at O'Connell Street. Fr Michael Harty in Maynooth had suggested he meet with Kevin Coffey, who was captain of Clanna Gael.

Coffey, a son of Beaufort, had won his first All-Ireland medal at centre-back in 1959 and added a second in '62. He would die too young in St Luke's Hospital in Rathgar, at 48 years of age, after giving further service to Dublin with the Kilmacud Crokes club.

It was a great relief to have made the decision to leave Maynooth, but living with it was helped as others like Kevin Coffey offered him advice on how to take the next steps in life. Tomás O Fiaich advised and urged him to talk to Mícheál Ó'Súilleabháin, who offered him words of wisdom, though on the blunt side.

'Mícheál told me, "Don't be looking back… burn your bridges!"

'I found that such good advice.

'He was very kind and helpful to me over the years, as was Tomás. Tomás O Fiaich was always close to us as students, not just teaching us history, but helping us in so many ways. He was a wonderful man, and he never changed.'

Donie's new 'home' in Dublin was a welcoming, kindly and generous one, where he lived with Paddy, Maggie and Seán Poole. The accommodation was arranged through Jimmy Fleming and Batt Garvey, who sought out a 'strong GAA house' for the young Kerryman.

DUBLIN ALWAYS HAD a huge influx of GAA players from more rural areas, for work or study, and clubs attracted them as much by profession as geography.

You played with the people you interacted with on a daily basis; that was just common sense. It simply happened that a rural agricultural people, i.e. most of Ireland, tended to live where they made a living, but that wasn't true of an urban population.

Seán Ó Síocháin had captained Clanna Gael to their first Dublin championship in 1936. By the early-60s, the former Cork and Dublin player had left teaching to work full-time for the GAA. Ó Síocháin was a regular singer and GAA commentator and spokesman on the radio, and an iconic figure.

He would replace Padraig Ó Caoimh as secretary (later the post would be renamed Director General) of the GAA in 1964.

The Ringsend club were not the dominant outfit in Dublin; that was unquestionably St Vincent's, but it was a major power all the same. Paddy Holden was the Dublin centre-back and one of the best-known footballers in the country. Mickey Whelan, who would later, like Donie, learn a lot about coaching and tactics by absorbing information from other codes in the US, was a highly rated forward long before he became known as one of the best managers of a generation. Gerry Davy, Chris Kane, Aidan Donnelly and Tony Gillee were all Dublin footballers.

In the 1963 county championship, Clanna Gael caused a big shock when they defeated St Vincent's in the semi-final. In the final they drew with UCD, who had a host of stars involved – Kerrymen Paud O'Donoghue and Mick O'Shea, George Kane (Westmeath), Eddie Melvin (Mayo), Paul Kelly (Donegal), Seán Murray (Longford), Bernard Brady (Donegal) and Séamus Hayden (Leitrim).

In the replay, which went out to early 1964, Man of the Match was unanimous; Donie gave one of his best performances... he was simply unbeatable. But his team wasn't.

Clanna Gael went down by 2-12 to 2-8 in a thriller.

UCD would add another championship title in 1965. Clanna Gael would have to wait until 1968 to claim theirs, with a team that included Mickey Whelan, Gerry Davey, Mick Byrne (future FAI physio) and Kerry natives Timothy Lyne, Pat O'Connell, Tadhg O'Donoghue and team captain Mossie O'Driscoll (all Valentia), Thady O'Donoghue (Firies) and James McGill (Ardcost).

IT WAS THE year of the big freeze.

The Sem was closed for the duration in 1963; instead, lads went and cycled between Ross and Innisfallen islands on Loch Léin on the frozen ice. This was also the year that Princess Grace, the Beatles, and most notably John Fitzgerald Kennedy, as stated, all came to Ireland. The country had a more cosmopolitan feel about it now. The economy was growing, thanks to Seán Lemass trusting the 1958 Report on Economic Development produced by TK Whitaker, Secretary of the Department of Finance in 1958 for the new Government.

Liebherr, the German crane manufacturers, had agreed to build a factory in Fossa, just outside Killarney in 1958 – they would remain huge employers in the town.

Emigration was slowing perceptibly (but still high compared to other countries). Employment was increasing as grants and tax exemptions were used to encourage manufacture for export.

The standard of living had remained stagnant in real terms in the 1950s, but in the 60s GDP increased by 4.4 percent per annum, economic openness grew by 23 percent, and unemployment averaged just over five percent. That was a rapid turnaround. Radios, televisions, and cars were available and, for an increasing amount of people, affordable.

KERRY WENT THE distance in the National League.

The final drew a huge crowd and saw them, aided by a strong breeze and 0-3 apiece from Tom Long and Bernie O'Callaghan, lead Down by 0-9 to 1-0 at half-time. Kerry had obvious reasons for wanting to beat Down at this stage, after the two All-Ireland defeats in 1960 and '61, but Brian Johnston, Tony Hadden and Paddy Doherty had no intention of going down quietly. Kevin Coffey and Tim 'Tiger' Lyons brilliantly hold off a late surge.

That win was a huge boost to Kerry's confidence.

'Looking back, it might have been the worst thing that could have happened to us,' says Donie, who had found himself in the wars a week before the final, after a 'late' tackle in a game with Clanna Gael left him in the Mater Hospital suffering from concussion and a broken nose. We would have been better off losing in the long term. It would have steeled us; we would have been able to respond better when Galway asked the harder questions later on.'

A rejigged Kerry huffed and puffed their way to a half-time deficit against Cork in Munster but the game settled into an enthralling tit-for-tat duel. The deadlock was broken when Tom Long laid off to Mick O'Dwyer bearing down on goal. 1-18 to 3-7 in the finish.

The semi-final against Galway attracted a disappointing crowd of 37,000 – television couldn't take all the blame, given that 70,000 turned up to see Dublin beat Down well. There is an old belief that Kerry supporters are so confident of All-Ireland semi-finals that they tend to save for the final – the evidence gives it some credence, at least.

Kerry cruised into an easy 0-4 to 0-1 lead (Mick O'Connell would finish with a personal tally of 0-7). They had turned it into a 0-7 to 0-2 lead early in the second-half. Then Galway got an opportunistic goal from Pat Donnellan, and suddenly the Tribesmen could sniff a weakness.

Mattie McDonagh started directing traffic, and two late points by Seamus Leyden saw Galway go through. They hadn't quite got the spring to get past a hard-bodied Dublin obstacle in the final, going down 1-9 to 0-10, but in Galway the west was definitely waking.

IN 1964, THE death penalty was abolished for all crimes, except murder of a garda, diplomat or prison officer. Templemore, the gardaí training barracks, opened its doors for the first time, as did the US Embassy in Dublin. Seán Ó Síocháin replaced Padraig Ó Caoimh as General Secretary of the GAA – Con Murphy, Maurice Hayes, Liam Hastings and Kevin Heffernan had all applied for the job.

Kerry lost out to Galway in the National League 'Home' final in 1965, with Galway subsequently beating New York. That prize of a trip to the States was a big one and it was alleged (and allegations persist to this day) that Mattie McDonogh lifted the ball off the ground illegally before setting up Seamus Leydon for the winning goal late on. Two of Kerry's sons answer all the critics in style. Dr Jim Brosnan, chairman of the county board, and Padraig 'PF' Foley of *The Kerryman* immediately disassociate Kerry from all such reports in the national papers and generously congratulate Galway on their victory.

This is Kerry, and this is how it is done.

Munster was surprisingly comfortable. Kerry ran through a soft campaign and opened with a goal from Tom Long against Cavan. That set them on their way as they ran out convincing winners, 2-12 to 1-7.

Time to put Galway back in their box. The only problem was that no-one gave Galway the script and they produced scintillating football in the All-Ireland final. Cyril Dunne racked up a 0-9 tally (to Mick O'Connell 0-7) and Galway sliced Kerry open repeatedly with fast, free-flowing football.

Kerry had one last chance as John Joe Barrett flung a thunderbolt at the Galway goal, but Johnny Geraghty sprang across and caught the lightning in his hand. John Donnellan lifted the cup as captain, something his father, a great player, captain, and subsequently TD had never gotten to do. Sadly, Mick Donnellan passed away in the stand before seeing his son lift the trophy.

John had his brother Pat, Galway's midfield engine, beside him. Years later, in 2001, John's own sons Michael and John would be part of a victorious Galway team.

John Mitchels' long reign in Kerry finally came to an end in the county quarter-final at the hands of South Kerry. That left the door open for East Kerry to reach the final against Shannon Rangers, but a formidable East Kerry were still missing a few key players.

One of them was Donie – and he was a big loss in their defeat to a great Shannon Rangers side, who would go on to win the first Munster Club Championship.

East Kerry, including their Dr Crokes' contingent, were still waiting for a county title, but they were learning lessons and edging closer all the time. The following year, with Donie O'Sullivan imperious at centre-back, it would be a different story.

YOU NAME IT Johnny Culloty played it.

And he was good at *anything* he played. He has never counted his medals; you'd have a full day's work in the job. Not that it ever bothered him too much.

When it comes to your sport in Kerry, you will be measured by football first. And Johnny was a great footballer. Never big, but he had phenomenal skill and agility. The ball stuck to him like glue and he would simply glide past markers – it was as if he could lower his centre of gravity at will.

He was a prodigy from a young age. He won senior and minor basketball All-Irelands with Kerry in the one year in the early-50s; basketball was fairly new around the town but it was fantastic for kids. An indoor game with speed, excitement, high scoring, and the occasional chance to bash into each other? It was also exotic, a part of an American culture that they normally only saw in Tommy Cooper's cinema. Of course, the town kids took to it like ducks to water.

Again, the truth is that it wasn't viewed as a threat to GAA, and that counted for a lot. It would keep them fit during the winter. It wasn't a field sport, so didn't need the same facilities, and it was played indoors; it didn't clash with football games.

'Johnny was in St Brendan's, and he was so good at everything… you heard about him before you even saw him,' recalls Donie.

'Football was his number one passion, but he was exceptional as a basketball player, and he was an outstanding hurler. He was a great guide to me too, and I listened because I knew what Johnny was saying was always right.

'In 1970, we were playing Derry in the semi-final and they were steam-rolling us early on. Every time Johnny placed the ball for me, for the kick-out, we would often have a few words.

'We'd have our little chat, and he would give me some advice on what was happening. I remember him saying to me, after he placed the ball… "If we can prevent them getting a goal, we can still win this!"

'A little while later, he saved a penalty, and if that penalty had gone in, it was over… we would never have come back.'

Johnny was a point guard on the basketball court. He directed the plays and made the key passes – game intelligence, you see. He's still one of the best judges of a game around Killarney – but he's not going to tell you that.

Himself and his brother Mickey were a rarity in Killarney – they loved the hurling. In fact, Johnny might be famous for football, because in Kerry it's football that makes you famous, but if anything, he has a deeper grá for the hurling. He was 15 when he stood in goal for the Kerry minor hurlers.

It wasn't that he was a natural goalkeeper.

Johnny actually played in the forwards, but he was young for midfield. That was 1951. The Kerry minors were drawn against Limerick for their annual drubbing in the Munster Championship. And yes, that's what they got… this isn't any fairytale.

The Kerry goalkeeper was kept busy during the game, of course; there was always going to be a disparity between the sides. But the young lad stood up to the task and gave it everything. One of the Limerick supporters was impressed and told him so afterwards. It's quite possible that Mick Mackey was being kind; like a lot of the tough hurlers, Mackey was known to be a very kind man off the field.

But it was no small thing for a hurler of Mick Mackey's renown to say that to a kid.

Johnny played centre-forward for the Kerry minors in 1954. A good team. Tim Barrett, Jack Dowling from Castlegregory, Brendan Kennelly, Frank O'Leary and Tom Garvey from Dingle, Tom Long, Teddy O'Dowd, Fred Lynch, and Brian Sheehy from Mitchels.

They hammered Cork in the Munster final and were cruising against Dublin in the final… 1-8 to 1-3 with a minute left. Dublin had Vinnie Bell, who was probably the highest rated minor the country had seen to that point.

Paddy Farnan got a Dublin goal. Injury time then, and a Dublin free. Vinnie Bell centred it, and Aidan Kavanagh fisted home… 3-3 to 1-8. Dublin were All-Ireland champions. A hard lesson for young Johnny Culloty; he would take it on board. A year later he would again play for Kerry against Dublin. This was one of the most famous meetings between the two, a game that is still talked about to this day.

There are a hundred stories about that game, and a 15-year-old Donie knew them as well as anybody else. In Kerry, how could you not? Nineteen-year-old Johnny Culloty was already a prodigy, but soon, the wily corner-forward would become a legend.

Not that Johnny cared too much about that, then or now.

He loved the games, has loved them with a gentle passion all his life, but he never mistook them for anything other than games.

◄ ◄ ◆ ► ►

JOHNNY CULLOTY

I played a lot of sports growing up, we all did. We would try our hand at anything. My main sport, curiously enough, was always hurling. Killarney actually had a very good minor team in the early-50s, thanks to people like Ben Campion.

I was in goal for the Kerry minors well before I ever got a call to join the footballers. I was very young… I hurled from 1949 up to 1971.

We had fantastic days. I remember us being beaten by Galway in a semi-final. I won an All-Ireland junior in 1961; that was a very big deal for Kerry hurling. I remember we played Kilkenny in another junior final in Thurles; Denis Heaslip lined out for Kilkenny that day. They had some fabulous hurlers.

I played in six Division Two finals, and we won two of them. They would have been curtain-raisers. I wasn't the only footballer on the team. Big Niall Sheehy would hardly miss a game. At that time, charging the goalkeeper was commonplace, but there weren't many got past Niall in either football or hurling!

His father John Joe would be at most of our games as well.

He would give a pep talk before the game and often at half-time. He was a great judge of a game, the same as he was in football. Of course, John Joe had been a great hurler for Mitchels and Kerry himself in his playing days.

I started going to matches in the 1940s. You had a lot of Kerry fellas interned then. Johnny Riordan was the Kerry goalkeeper; a good keeper and a fantastic entertainer. I remember him walking across the goal on his hands, I had never seen anything like it. All the Kerry supporters would love it. John Joe Sheehy would be on the hill watching… he wouldn't be quite as impressed!

You have to understand that Dr Eamonn had very little say in things. He certainly had no say in picking the team; that would have been unthinkable. John Joe was with Kerry as a player and selector from the late 20s to the early-60s. Johnny Walsh was there for years, Paddy Bawn… Murt Kelly.

What they said went.

They lived Kerry football and they called the shots.

Dr Eamon trained Kerry teams from 1926 to '62, he wasn't involved much later. I had a number of different trainers after that, Dr Jim Brosnan and Johnny Walsh among them.

They were completely different times.

We'd never heard of physios or dieticians in the early days. Ollie Brown would give us a rub-down – Ollie was an All-Ireland boxing champion and a physio in Tralee. Dinso Hurley who worked in St Finan's, Mick Jennings of Mitchels, Rory O'Connell of Stacks… these people would take care of us, keep us going. All complete volunteers, never got the credit they deserved and certainly never got paid a penny; the county board wouldn't be paying any fella! Unheard of!

There was never a mention of a gym, either.

I came on as a sub in the Munster final in 1955, that was my first game for Kerry. You didn't train with Kerry. I don't think I ever remember a training session for a National League game. You looked after yourself through club games and the like. For the final we trained for three weeks under Dr Eamonn.

There was no compensation, no travel expenses... none of that. I think the county board would pay for substitutes for the teachers on the panel; that was all.

I worked in St Finan's Hospital from 1956 to 2002. At that time, you'd start off on night duty for three months. There was no extra pay for Saturdays, Sundays, or night work. Lads were usually willing to swap when I had a game on Sunday; I would work a weekday instead for them. I had to pay someone to do my shift often enough, though.

You didn't get any favours from Dr Eamonn on account of being a Kerry footballer; there was no interaction like that at work.

It was completely separate from the football. We trained with Dr Eamonn twice a day in a training camp. We stayed in the Sem; it used to be Scott's Hotel before my time... Mrs. Scott took great care of the players. Everything was regulated – walks, field training, a bit of golf. Religion was certainly not forgotten.

There would be Mass daily... and the rosary was said. In later years after training nights, we would go down to the Park Place Hotel, where Mickey Doc (a son of Dr Paddy O'Donoghue and a huge supporter of Kerry football) would always make sure that we were well fed.

During my time in St Finan's, I met a lot of patients who had been involved in building the Fitzgerald Stadium. The hill was solid then. Dr Eamonn was very big into getting the patients out. There were over 1,000 patients at that time.

The hospital had a farm up in Gortroe that the patients worked, and they loved it. When the Fitzgerald stadium was sodded, farmers would grow a patch of sod up where the Killarney Legion Pitch is now, up in Derreen. The patients would cut it up with spades, roll it up, and it would be brought down to the Stadium where it could be rolled into place. I met many patients who had been in St Finan's in the 30s. They mostly came from farms, they had been doing that sort of work all their lives. It didn't just occupy them; it made them feel useful.

We would tog out for Munster finals in Killarney in St Finan's; there was one big shed at either side and one of those was the Kerry dressing-room. Cork would tog out in The Imperial; it's now the Killarney Towers Hotel.

Donie came in with Kerry in 1962.

I knew him before that, of course, from playing with Crokes. His brother Tim was playing with the hospital team at that time, and there were a lot of footballers from out his way... the likes of Johnny and Denny Doolan, John Kelly, Pat Casey, Tim Kelly.

Legion won East Kerry from 1952 to '54, but Dr Crokes took over after that and dominated the competition from 1956 well into the 60s. They were a great team, in fairness. You had Tom Long and Donie, great footballers, and they had very good forwards.

The one team they couldn't get past in those days was John Mitchels; that was a phenomenal club team.

The first thing anyone noticed about Donie was how he could kick the ball. It was incredible. Donie could land a kick-out past midfield... that was how much power he had.

He was definitely the longest kicker of the heavy ball that I ever saw for Kerry, or for anybody else. That was very important for Kerry. A lot of football was played that way... long direct kicking.

There was no dropping men back, you stayed within your sector and marked your man. The game has evolved since, but any game is always evolving.

There was more tactical awareness than people think nowadays. Defenders would talk to each other about how to cover particular dangers.

Of course, his kicking was his most famous trait, but Donie was a very good footballer anyway. He was best known as a defender but you could play Donie anywhere.

Dr Eamonn's mantra for defenders always was 'close continual coverage without fouling', and that always suited Donie down to the ground. He would go one-on-one with any player. He was very strong, too.

I remember when we played Dublin in the semi-final in 1962, Donie marked Kevin Heffernan, who was of course a deserved legend by then. Donie was a newcomer in just his second game for Kerry, but he comfortably had the better of him that day. That was the start of a brilliant career for Kerry.

We didn't win as much in the 60s as I think we could have. That's not disrespecting Galway, they were a tremendous outfit and had some brilliant players, but I never felt that Kerry produced their best in those years.

The likes of Jerdie O'Connor and Denis O'Sullivan never got an All-Ireland medal, and they were great footballers. The balance of the team was slightly off.

We had a lot of great defenders lining out as forwards. When you look at our scores against Galway, we never got a championship goal against them in those years.

After leaving Maynooth College, Donie played football with Clanna Gael in Dublin while teaching in the city. Here, after winning the Leinster Championship, are two of his teammates from those days, Paddy Holden (left) and Mickey Whelan (right), while in the centre is Kevin Heffernan.

Seán Ó'Síocháin, the future General Secretary of the GAA, played a significant role in Donie's Clanna Gael career.

« CHAPTER 8 »

BEN DUNNE SNR had already introduced a dramatic change in Irish retail shopping with his new type of stores in 1957. In these, you could browse through the rack and simply bring your selection to be paid for at a counter. You didn't have or need a consultation with an assistant; you simply picked out your own goods.

In 1965, already a retail giant, Dunne took another big step by building Ireland's first 'shopping centre'. You could buy all your goods within a short distance and a short amount of time. Families, more of whom were working regular hours and commuting to work, loved it.

Things were changing alright, but it was more of the same on the nation's greatest football stage. Once again, it was Kerry versus Dublin in Croke Park in an All-Ireland semi-final, and Dublin took a four-point lead in another cracker, but Mick O'Dwyer set up Derry O'Shea for an equalising goal, and Bernie O'Callaghan added another. The tide turned. In the end it was 4-8 to 2-6, and Donie had scored his first championship point for the county.

The final everybody wanted was at hand, Galway against Kerry, but it was not the result Kerry folk wished. Galway were just that little bit better. Joe Joe Barrett was unlucky to see a shot whizz just barely over the crossbar late in the first-half.

There had only ever been two sendings-off in an All-Ireland final prior to this, but Derry and John 'Thorny' O'Shea became famous when Thorny followed his brother's red card from referee (and future GAA president) Mick Loftus and got road late on; Galway's John Donnellan was also dismissed. It wasn't a fair reflection on what was a very sporting game.

A bad year by Kerry standards, but Donie himself had played very well. When the Cúchulainn Awards (the precursor of the All Stars) were announced, there were two Kerrymen on the team.

Mick O'Connell in midfield… and Donie O'Sullivan in the backs.

KERRY MINOR TIM Kelliher had 1-5 for the victorious Mid Kerry side, including a spectacular late goal, in an absolute thriller of a county semi-final versus the mighty Mitchels. East Kerry on the other hand had taken what was considered an easier route, having beaten St Brendan's and Ballymacelligott before a narrow, but fully deserved, semi-final victory over St Vincent's (a North Kerry amalgamation). East Kerry had the first three points in the final.

Mid Kerry only got the ball into the East Kerry half once in the opening 10 minutes – Donie sent out a message of intent as he coolly caught and cleared it. In the 11th minute, he also sent a beautiful long kick into Mick Gleeson, who neatly rolled it into the net. Mid Kerry brought Pat Griffin out to midfield in a swap with Jimmy Lucey and it proved a shrewd move. East Kerry led by 1-4 to 0-5 at half-time.

Mid Kerry, now with the strong wind, edged in to a 0-8 to 1-4 lead but a trademark huge kick into the Mid Kerry square by Donie saw Johnny Culloty fist off the crossbar, before Pat Cahill goaled from the rebound. DJ Crowley added another, and the game looked done and dusted when Gerard Cullinane hit the net.

After 50 minutes, East Kerry were seven points clear – 4-5 to 0-10 – and looked home and hosed. But Mid Kerry are one of those teams that never give up the ghost and they kept going.

Weeshie Fogarty made a good catch, but was shouldered over the line by Kevin Griffin. Tim Kelliher volleyed home a spectacular shot a minute later. Suddenly, the gap was down to a point and East Kerry were hanging on.

Pat Griffin, one of the best Kerry players of his era, managed to fist over an equaliser – Pat, who had incredible balance to match his pace, was almost impossible to stop in full flight. 4-5 to 2-11… a draw.

East Kerry laboured early on in the replay. Despite having a very strong wind in their favour, it was 0-1 apiece after 16 minutes, but then they cut the proverbial dogs loose. The second quarter saw them fire over seven points without reply.

The second-half was low-scoring. Donie, along with Pat Moynihan, Donal 'Socky' Lynch, Tom Long and Johnny Culloty came in for particular praise afterwards, but all accounts agree that it was East Kerry's teamwork and intelligence as a unit that made the real difference.

County champions, and East Kerry's first ever title.

It wouldn't be their last.

A FEW WISE heads were watching that East Kerry team from the background. It started as quiet speculation. A hint dropped here and there among the people who established the now defunct club called Spa.

There were Spa footballers worth looking at… *maybe*! Donie O'Sullivan, arguably the best defender in the country at that time. He had recently been awarded a Gaelic Sports All Star Award, after all. Pat Cahill – there have been Cahills, Caseys, and Cronins scattered throughout the area from time immemorial, and every one of them could play football.

Mick Gleeson wasn't a county player yet, but everyone who watched the 1965 championship knew that he would be, and word was that his younger brother Jim had all the makings of a footballer too. Jim had been a key player for the East Kerry minors who had won their own county championship in 1965.

There were some good young lads around the area.

More importantly, the economic renewal meant that there was a good chance that they wouldn't need to take a boat across the waters to earn a living… so, conversations, and hopes and doubts, abounded.

AH, NO. HOLD your horses a small bit.

Look, I'd love it. We're steeped in football, but we tried before and we didn't have enough footballers in the finish.

Our hearts can say what they want, but it's our heads that make decisions. One day we'll have a Spa club. I've seen the lads playing with Scoil Mhuire in the School League and there's always a friendly game being organised… somewhere in Spa, but you're getting carried away.

Maybe I'm not.

St Finan's aren't fielding next year.

There will be a few lads looking for a club to play with next year. And Spa would make a grand one for them.

St Finan's? Are you serious?

Sure, they had great footballers. Didn't Paudie O'Sullivan play for them? Seán Kelliher down below Lissivigeen Cross. Timmy Joe O'Sullivan, of course. Some man, Timmy Joe… we're lucky to have him for a neighbour. They reached the O'Donoghue Cup final two years ago and they gave Crokes plenty of it in the final.

I know, yeah. Denny Doolan was in goal that day. Mick Kissane and Paddy Dennehy the corner-backs. Mick Gleeson and Pat Casey outside them. John Cahill from the Kerry junior, Tim Kelly of Ardanaenig and John Kelly of Coolcaslagh in the forwards.

Jaysus, fair enough, if those lads come on board… it could be worth looking at. There's the bones of a football team in that, sure enough.

You're forgetting Donie O'Sullivan.

That's a big ace in any hand.

Ah, yeah. But look, isn't he playing for some crowd in Dublin.

Clanna Gael? And he has two O'Donoghue Cup medals with Crokes. They aren't far away, you know. Mitchels aren't what they were, and Crokes and Donie will both know that. No… a big name footballer like Donie O'Sullivan will play with a big club.

That's human nature. And if he rejoins Crokes, you can bet that a lot of lads from St Finan's will follow suit.

That'd make sense, I'll grant you.

But let me turn that on its head. You know Donie the same as I do. True enough that a lot of lads will follow on if he plays for someone else. But what are the odds of Donie lining out against any of those lads?

Against Spa?

Donie O'Sullivan?

Ask him yourself. Donie is backing this all the way and he's saying that to anyone who asks.

I didn't look at it that way.

D'you know, either you have a fair point, or I have a drink too many taken. It would be worth a try. Maybe it'd be no harm if a decent man like yourself could have

a small word with Timmy Joe O'Sullivan… or Tadhg O'Sullivan?
Who do you think suggested that I have a word with you?

THERE WAS NO one particular moment.

Spa had always been a kind of an idea born and bred into the character of the community on a subconscious level.

The same is true of any sports club that ever existed; you had to have a core group involved in playing before you could germinate a club. Spa pre-existed it's foundation in 1948 and continued long after it apparently folded in the early-60s. Tadhg O'Sullivan and Timmy Joe O'Sullivan were the catalysts, no question about it, but they had been ploughing the harrows and sowing the seeds.

The conversations around re-forming in 1965 were not the start of the planting; they were the preparations for the harvest.

The club held an AGM in early February in 1966, once again in the old Macra na Feirme Hall (it was straight across the road from Lissivigeen NS). Tadhg O'Sullivan was elected chairman, with Denis Fenton as secretary and Denny Doolan as treasurer. The club received a percentage of Ciste na mBan pools that cost one shilling a week, while Spa membership cost half a crown.

Tadhg O'Sullivan, Timmy Joe, and John 'Dunn' O'Donoghue had a training programme that was strict enough by the standards of the time – Spa were not going into this with half measures.

They played Currow in their first game, a challenge match.

A win was hugely significant. Not just because Spa had shown that they could go up against a serious team. Make no mistake, a Currow side that had the likes of Mike Galwey (All-Ireland winner and uncle of the genial rugby giant), Mick Aherne (Kerry minor in 1965 and junior in '66), Derry Mangan (Kerry junior) and 1963 minor Con Riordan was a very serious team. Dan Bawn O'Sullivan would go on to become a great referee and a much-loved icon of football in the county – everybody knew Dan Bawn and was the better for knowing him. Gene Brosnan, John Horan, and Johnny Scanlon had won a Vocational Schools All-Ireland in 1960.

Even in the absence of the likes of Moss Keane and the Doyle brothers, Mick and Tom because of rugby, any team that could stand up to Currow on the field wouldn't need to fear too many others. After all, Spa were missing some top guns themselves – Pat Casey (who would later play midfield for Kerry and would have featured much more but for his job), and Johnny Doolan were away on duty with the Irish navy, while Donie and Mick Gleeson were away studying. For Spa to beat a good team without these four was a strong message.

They lost to Listry in the opening game of the 1966 East Kerry League, but that was only a temporary blip. With the four lads back, they beat Rathmore by four points in the semi-final.

Dr Crokes had, of course, started the competition as reigning champions for the past two years and red-hot favourites. Their hopes were dashed early on when St Agatha's of Glenflesk put them to the sword.

Glenflesk were then expected to dispose of Kilcummin at their ease, and in fact took a 1-4 to 0-0 lead against the wind. It was 1-4 to 0-2 at half-time and looked all over, but Kilcummin rallied brilliantly to draw level. In the last quarter they added another four points for a big lead against the odds. Glenflesk got a late goal through Ger O'Donoghue but Kilcummin held out.

Timmy Joe O'Sullivan had a box of faded blue and gold jerseys from the team of the 40s and early-50s. It felt like an omen for Spa – they didn't have too many omens in their favour after that semi-final performance by Kilcummin!

Like Spa, Kilcummin had never won an O'Donoghue Cup. Eugene Moriarty trained that Kilcummin team. Billy Doolan and Dan Dwyer, two great Kilcummin stalwarts to this day and two highly respected judges of football, were East Kerry teammates of Donie's. Tim Sheehan, one of the five sons of Consie (four of whom played for Kilcummin that day), had won a junior All-Ireland in 1963 and played with Donie on the Kerry team within a year.

Kilcummin were confident.

Donie travelled down from Tiernaboul with Johnny Batt Cronin (teammate, pal, raconteur, a great Spa player and mentor, and a great friend to all and sundry who were lucky enough to know him) to play the O'Donoghue Cup final. You couldn't travel in better company.

Kilcummin were a very good team, and everybody attending the final knew it. But Spa were a good team as well, and I'm pretty sure that wasn't exactly a well-kept secret either. There were Kilcummin people helping their Spa neighbours the day before and after the game and vice versa.

They were opponents on the field, not enemies – it's a more profound difference that too many commentators fail to appreciate.

It was a tough game. Brothers Tim (who scored 0-5) and John Sheehan in midfield had a huge duel with Pat Casey and Tom Morris. Donie, who captained the team at centre-back, was the best of the many great players on the field. He kicked three second-half points, all of them from long distance. Joe Sheehan had no answer to Donie.

For that matter, Johnny Batt and Fr Michael on either side of the Spa captain were also outstanding. Brian Fenton, father of the current brilliant Dublin midfielder, had one of his many great games for the club. Spa's inside forward line of Paddy Dennehy, John Kelly and Seán Moynihan were superb. None of them were young, but they were all good footballers.

It was Paddy who cut in with a great run, having been put through by Mick Gleeson, and gave Kilcummin goalkeeper Pat O'Connor no chance midway through the second-half. That goal was decisive, with Man of the Match, Donie and Denny Doolan outstanding in the last quarter. The final score was Spa 1-11, Kilcummin 1-6.

Spa: Mick Kissane; Denny Doolan, Jack Morris, Jim Gleeson; Johnny Batt Cronin, Donie O'Sullivan, Fr Michael O'Donoghue; Pat Casey, Tom Morris; Brian Fenton, Mick Gleeson, Mickey Cronin; Seán Moynihan, Paddy Dennehy, John Kelly. Subs: John 'Dunn' O'Donoghue, Flossy McCarthy, Seanie Moynihan, Johnny Doolan, John Joe Foley, Dan Joe O'Sullivan, Denis Fenton.

IT WAS A huge marker laid down – check any Spa team then or since, and you'll see the surnames repeating.

The celebrations were probably as action-packed and boisterous as the game itself. There was one important phone call that had to be made along the way. Donie's brother, Fr Tim, was attending to his duties in Scunthorpe in England, waiting for word.

At 11pm, the parish priest informed him gently that there were 'rather boisterous people' on the phone. Fr Tim's reaction to the news meant that he had to explain what had happened.

And that's how a gentle and civilised priest and a Spanish Jesuit got an explanation, that included a comparison between England's World Cup folk hero Nobby Stiles and Spa's O'Donoghue Cup hero Johnny Batt Cronin... with Johnny Batt just tipping the scales.

Spa and Crokes played out a real thriller in the opening round of the championship, just one week after their O'Donoghue Cup win. Paddy Dennehy was again the hero, sending a brilliant 50-metre kick between the posts late on to snatch a one-point victory. The final was played on Easter Sunday in 1967 without Donie, who was in the US.

Gneeveguilla had great players – John Barry (still their popular county board delegate), the O'Keeffe's, Paddy and Aeneas O'Leary.... lion-hearted Jerry McCarthy, and stylish midfielder Pat Moynihan were county footballers. Weather conditions weren't great, but the football was high quality; it was simply a brilliant game.

Any lingering suspicion that Spa were a one-man team and vulnerable without their county star were laid permanently to rest. Goals by Mick Gleeson and Seán O'Sullivan in the first-half and John Kelly's 50th minute goal clinched victory.

It was Fr Tim who presented the medals at the Spa social in The Gleneagle Hotel that Christmas. He gave one player a miraculous medal instead of an O'Donoghue Cup one (around here, the two have pretty much the same currency anyway). When the player realised it (to much hilarity), the comment of the night had to go to Tom Fleming.

He stated with apparent innocence that Spa winning the O'Donoghue Cup could be considered a miracle in its own right – but the fact that the player in question had managed to kick two points against Listry should be subject to a Lourdes inquiry, because it certainly defied natural explanation!

Wearing the blue of East Kerry, and the green and gold of his home parish, were each a second skin for Donie. He had given his all every time he pulled on the Clanna Gael jersey, but there is something about a cloth that men in your own parish have worn on their backs before you.

And they had worn those jerseys in Spa… they were well worn. 'They had been hidden under a bed, I think, in Timmy Joe O'Sullivan's house for about 15 years!' Donie states with a chuckle. 'The colours were well faded, but they were our colours, still.

'It had been great to play with Clanna Gael, and it had been very convenient for me while I was in Dublin.'

Even though the journeys home to Spa, and back to Dublin to his teaching post, were long treks which ate deeply into any weekend.

'We were young, and every time it was an adventure.

'We could have opponents in the car with us; it was great enjoyment always, setting off home for a game.' Stiffness and soreness at the end of any one of those five- or six-hour journeys did not dim their enthusiasm.

'Sure, we were young and fit, and we had green grass awaiting us… and a white ball, wasn't that what life was about? We never thought about the journey back to Dublin the next morning.

'We did it out of love for the game, but also out of loyalty… we never questioned it.

'I remember, at the start of one summer, Mick Gleeson talking about maybe going to America, and I smiled at the idea. "No, you won't go!" I told him. "Because once Tadhg O'Sullivan phones you… you'll be there!"

'When Tadhg phoned us, we knew we were needed down home for a game, and in honesty we never took much persuading, if any at all. We were waiting for the phone calls most of the time.

'There was no demanding of us, and the lads at home knew we would never say no. They were also decent. They would give us our petrol money, because they knew we needed that to keep things going.

'We were well looked after but, more than anything… we were young and fit as I've said… what else would we want to be doing other than playing for Spa and East Kerry!

'Playing for the teams, and playing for Kerry… that's what it is all about, friendships, and memories of games. If we were young enough now, we would do it all over again… and be thankful to be able to do it.'

MICK GLEESON PLAYED gaelic football with Spa and was a member of the Kerry senior county team from 1969 until '72, winning two All-Irelands. He was also a member of the Kerry junior team and won an All-Ireland Junior Championship medal in 1967.

He won four Kerry Senior Football Championships, a Munster Senior Club Football Championship and an All-Ireland Senior Club Football Championship with East Kerry, when he was also team captain.

With Spa he won seven East Kerry Senior Football Championship titles (O'Donohue Cups) and a county Intermediate Football Championship. During his college days in Dublin, he won a Dublin Under 21 Football Championship with Erin's Hope in 1966. He later played with UCD and won a Sigerson Cup with them.

He spent pretty much all of his working life as a teacher in Monastery, across the road from St Brendan's College. Mick had the patience and natural kindness so necessary for teachers; no one has counted how many All-Ireland medallists have emerged from his classrooms; that was never the measure he had for them.

He was a Killarney town councillor from 1991 to 2014 and has been a Kerry County Councillor since 1999, as part of the Kerry Independent Alliance. He was within a handful of votes of being elected in the 2011 general election. He has also been Mayor of Killarney.

As a footballer Mick was big and strong, but he was also one of the fastest players on any pitch, in thought as well as body. He was a deadly goal-poacher and immensely skilful. He was also completely fearless.

Ironically for a footballer who would come to epitomise the Spa community, that wasn't where he first learned to play football.

◄ ◄ ◆ ► ►

MICK GLEESON

I went to secondary school in Ballyvourney and I played football regularly there. Not that we had any kind of a team to speak of, but we played a couple of times a week in bPairc an Choláiste. We played in all schools' competitions including Corn na Mumhan and failed dismally. This was very much contrary to the years before us in the 1950s when Coláiste Íosagáin was the top college in Munster with players like Seamus Murphy and Tom Long, who were among the great college players of that era.

Unfortunately, from 1960 to '64 during my years there, we didn't really have much football talent and there was literally no interest from the president of the college, so overall we were very unsuccessful. We won just one competition in all that time... the Simcox Cup, which was for Cork colleges. We beat Chríost Rí from Cork city in the final and they had a number of good quality players.

I would have been totally unaware of Spa as a child. It didn't exist on my radar. The Spa club went out of existence in the early-50s. I was born in September, 1945, so when it ceased to exist, I would only have been about six or seven. I wouldn't have known about it and even if I had, its focal point would have been at the other end of the area from where we lived in Minish.

Our only journeys then would have been in the horse and trap to Mass in Killarney on a Sunday and I didn't know anything about the area generally known as Spa.

I played a lot of football, of course. in Lissivigeen National School. When I was there, I played in goal with Naomh Mhuire, the local primary schools' team. The amalgam of the schools from East Kerry won the county schools championship in 1958. That was my first team triumph.

I practised and played football at home with my brothers often when the farming work after school was done.

Interestingly enough, my father, who had very little interest in the game, came home from town after a fair day and said that Pat O'Meara asked if I would play with the Legion. (Pat O'Meara was a founder of the Legion club and a hugely respected figure in Killarney). Now, I didn't know Legion from Crokes but I was delighted to be asked and afforded an opportunity to play.

In 1958 and '59, I played minor county championship football in goal for the Legion. Weeshie Fogarty was the Kerry minor goalkeeper at the time, but in club championship games both years he played outfield.

In September of 1959 until the following Easter, I went to school in Dingle to prepare for an exam called the Preparatory Exam in Scoil na mBráthar. Liam Higgins, later a county colleague and dear friend was a classmate. There were two teams in Dingle at that time, John St and Na Piarsaigh, and I would have been in John St territory. I never formally played competitively with them, but I played challenge games with them.

In the early 1960s, there was a minor amalgamation between Spa and Glenflesk in East Kerry. In 1963, we had quite a good team and won the East Kerry Championship. It was only after very high interventions by a Franciscan friar that I was allowed out of Coláiste Íosagáin to play in that final.

That is an indication of the lack of interest by the president of Coláiste Íosagáin at the time. Winning the championship was a big boost for us young players. Following on from 1963, a number from that minor team who would become Spa players in 1966 played for St Finan's, reaching an O'Donoghue Cup final in 1964, when we were beaten by Dr Crokes.

In 1965, I went to St Patrick's Training College in Dublin where we played a considerable amount of football, We had quite good teams for the two years that I was there. We got to the Dublin senior semi-final in both years and we won the under-21 county title in 1966.

We were captained in 1965-66 by Brian McCarthy from Ballylongford, a very gifted footballer. He won Kerry championships with Shannon Rangers, as did his brother John.

Brian was actually captain of Ballybunion Golf Club when Bill Clinton came to visit. He insisted on playing a game with Clinton and he was right to do so. There were politicians demanding the privilege of playing with President Clinton but Brian insisted that the members be represented by him, their captain and in the end they played a five-ball which is a most unusual occurrence.

Pierse Lyne from Beara, a first cousin of Brian's, was in the Training College at that time, as was John Gibbons from Mayo. John played minor, under-21 and senior football, as well as junior and senior hurling for Mayo all in the one year. Also, on the team of 1965-66 was Liam Mulvihill who later became Árd Stiúrthóir of the GAA. It was during his term that the wonderful new Croke Park was developed.

I would argue that it was the college teams, UCD and Erin's Hope (which was the Training College's club name) and Clanna Gael and Civil Service, which were largely comprised of country players, that helped to keep football alive in Dublin during the 1950s and 60s. At that time the St Vincent's club had a Dublin natives-only policy.

At the end of the year in St Pat's there was the annual farewell dress dance which virtually everybody attended. The county semi-final in both years was played on the following evening which wasn't exactly ideal for the students. I think we could have won one year but there were a lot of great players with St Vincent's at the time... Lar Foley and his brother the superb Des, Kevin Heffernan, Tony Hanahoe, Jimmy Keaveney and Gay O'Driscoll.

As a result of playing with St Finan's, I was fortunate to play with East Kerry in 1964. I wasn't selected for the county final, where we were beaten by Shannon Rangers whose team included the aforementioned Brian McCarthy, as well as Jerdie O'Connor, Eamonn and Paud O'Donoghue and Dan McAuliffe, all of whom were county players then or later.

1965 was a seminal year for me. East Kerry reached the county final and we played Mid Kerry. I was lucky to score a miraculous goal - I think 'fluke' would be the *modern phrase, that helped us to draw the game! We won the replay. I played a few league games for Kerry later that year and then fell from favour.*

East Kerry had some fine players including Donie, Tom Long, Johnny Culloty, Pat Moynihan, Donal Lynch and many more. The following year we were beaten by John Mitchels of Tralee by a goal. They were a very good club side. They had a very special charisma about them, but I think the main thing they had was they were a very even bunch of players, rather than dependent on exceptional stars.

While I was in Dublin in 1966, around March or early April, somebody told me that a group of people had gotten together in the general Spa area and had re-formed the club and that they had already played some East Kerry games with mixed success. The team then defeated Gneeveguilla, and that was really a big win as it allowed the team to progress to the knockout stages.

When I came home at Easter holidays I was asked if I would play with them and I said I would of course. I heard that Donie O'Sullivan would also be playing with his own area. This was a big move for Donie as he was a very successful Dr Crokes player but the transfer was facilitated by the generosity and understanding of a great Dr Crokes player and mentor, Jackie Looney.

The campaign we had in 1966 was quite incredible, culminating in Paddy Dennehy's wonderful goal to seal victory for us against Kilcummin. It established the credibility of our club in both East Kerry and in the county.

Not only did it result in a victory for the club, but also in a resurrection for an entire community. That has remained vibrantly true ever since and shows how important the GAA is in enhancing the well-being of community.

It has given people a place to mix in a community setting. I think Spa GAA club is recognised now not just within Kerry but throughout most of the country and that is because of those who came together in 1966 to re-form the club.

I am forever grateful, as are my extended family and the wider Spa community that we have our own club. Its re-emergence has united, enriched and inspired.

In October in 1968, I started doing a BA at night in UCD Earlsfort Terrace while teaching in St Fergal's School in Finglas West. Donie was teaching in Blanchardstown. Jim Tunney, later Fianna Fail TD and Ceann Comhairle was the school principal.

Donie was doing a Diploma in Public Administration at the time in UCD. We both joined the college GAA club. As was the tradition, the Sigerson was fixed for

November. Our captain was Benny Gaughran from Dundalk. He was an outstanding player with club, county and province.

Our trainer was the late Eugene McGee, who in 1982 managed Offaly to All Ireland glory. We trained at 7.30am in Belfield, which could have been a huge challenge for someone living in Glasnevin on the other side of the city.

But our captain Benny would come every morning on his scooter at seven o'clock to Glasnevin to pillion me for the hour's training in Belfield. He would then return me to Harte's Corner from where I got the bus to school. He was a very genuine, generous man. Fate intervened, however, when there was an outbreak of Foot and Mouth disease in England and the Sigerson was deferred until the last week in February. We beat UCG in the final in Croke Park. Winning the Sigerson was very special for Donie and I.

Unfortunately, the powers-that-be, The Universities Council, introduced a rule prohibiting night students from participating in the Sigerson competition. That greatly aggrieved me and I went to Croke Park to make my protest – myself and John Gibbons of Mayo and Meath fame. We sat down with Seán Ó Siocháin, but we got little or no hearing. I think you could say that we were summarily dismissed. We could not understand why we were excluded. I'm still annoyed, even at this stage of my life. I continued to play with UCD in the Dublin championship and league for the duration of my studies.

I won a junior All-Ireland in 1967 when Kerry defeated London in the final in New Eltham. The Kerry juniors were beaten two years later by Wicklow, whose goalkeeper was Pat Cronin from the Stratford-on-Slaney club. He convinced me to train them and they won the Wicklow Junior Championship in 1971, their third time reaching the final and first ever win.

I remember a series of articles in The Kerryman newspaper during the 1960s asking 'What's Wrong with Kerry Football'. A different person contributed each week. One of the contributors was Jackie Lyne and as a result of his article he was appointed by Dr Jim Brosnan to become trainer of the Kerry team.

East Kerry won three County Championships – 1968, '69 and '70 and I was lucky to captain them that final season, which meant that I was captain of the team as it faced into the first-ever All-Ireland Club Championship. East Kerry defeated Bryansford of Down in the final comprehensively. We had a very good team

Unfortunately, I think our All Ireland club victory sealed the fate of divisional teams in the club championship, even though there is no such thing as a parish rule in many counties such as Dublin. I always thought that it was a great pity that players from very scattered and peripheral areas such as South Kerry, Duhallow and West Kerry are not get an opportunity to represent their area in the senior club championship when they become champions of their own county.

Spa went on to win more O'Donoghue Cups in East Kerry and Donie O'Sullivan would have been a dominant figure in those games. His power and his commitment were a great affirmation to the other players, as was the fact that he was almost always available.

He was a wonderful clubman even though for a lot of that time he and I were domiciled in Dublin. I had no car. I was completely dependent on him or else the train, but Donie rarely if ever missed a game.

That was so important to the local players, that their star player Donie O'Sullivan was always available… big games, small games, even carnival games which were a big thing at the time. They probably kept the club alive financially in its earlier years. He was always there, except for an educational sojourn in New York in the mid-60s. He was inspirational for us all.

I remember Donie, myself, and Eamonn Fitzgerald of Dr Crokes coming down to play an East Kerry final in 1968. The game was fixed for seven o'clock on a Friday evening. I recall that we got out of the car at Gleannsharoun overlooking Castleisland to try to loosen our limbs for the game.

Our colleagues, and Eamonn's teammates, were togged out and ready to take the field before we even got to the dressing-rooms. You can't play a game after five hours in a car. Dr Crokes were victorious and the victory gave them the right to name the captain of Kerry for the following year. As they had no player on the county team they gave the honour to Johnny Culloty of Killarney Legion, a great player who won his first All-Ireland in 1955. Johnny led Kerry to its 21st title in September, 1969, when we defeated Offaly on the score 0-10 to 0-7.

Following the 1966 O'Donoghue Cup victory, Spa remained one of the top clubs in East Kerry for many years. The commitment was huge and in the early and mid-70s we had a very good sides and one year progressed to the quarter-final of the county championship. The club won a total of seven divisional titles in little over a decade.

Spa was a small and fairly sparsely populated area in the 1960s, as distinct from now when there are far more homes.

Those who took that chance in 1966 have had a great influence on our lives. We are hugely proud of that community and all that it has achieved. It places an enormous obligation on all of us to ensure that the area and the club continue to prosper and remain reasonably successful both on and off the field. Those must always be our objectives.

I am deeply grateful to have had some part in Spa's triumphs and in the continued development of the locality. Grateful also to have shared in much that was vibrant and enriching for club and community with Donie O' Sullivan .

Guím rath agus séan ort, Donie, ar do chlann 's do gharchlann. Go maire tú an chéad.

◄◄◆►►

IN 1966, DONOGH O'Malley announced that secondary education in Ireland would be free. It was a seismic change – in 1966 just 36 percent of 16 year olds were still in education. O'Malley announced it an NUJ dinner without consulting his government or Department of Education colleagues, cleverly getting all the political credit.

It had, in fact, been developed and planned for several years.

Nelson's Pillar on Sackville Street was blown up by the IRA as part of the 50th anniversary of the Easter Rising. The Irish public were relatively pleased overall as the pillar had long been considered an anachronism at best.

Ireland's anti-English stance had mellowed somewhat, though, and England's hosting and triumph in the World Cup saw the fairly narrow urbanised support for soccer widen considerably. Mick O'Connell, who had played the game as a boy with Spanish trawlermen who visited Valentia, always had an admiration for the skill of the game.

Cassius Clay had recently changed his name to the more suspicious Muhammad Ali. In 1966, a lot of people wanted Cleveland Williams or Henry Cooper to knock him out – they failed.

Nothing could come close to Pat Taaffe on the legendary Arkle either, as he won his third Gold Cup on the trot. Jack Nicklaus became the fourth person to win all four majors after winning the British Open. Billie Jean King won Wimbledon.

It was also the year that Pretty Polly opened in Killarney.

Oh, it was officially the Killarney Hosiery Company and the name changed on occasion over the years; I think it was the Sara Lee Factory at the finish. But it was the 'Pretty Polly' factory to people in Killarney, and at its height it employed over 900 of them. Along with Liebherr and Hilliard's Boot Factory, it was a huge employer.

Remember that journey up to the Spa field at the start of this book?

When you turned left at the roundabout instead of continuing out the Cork Road? Just up there on your left, before the entrance to the Ballyspillane housing estate, is the Pretty Polly factory.

Sadly, it has been closed since 2005.

While industry was growing in Killarney, it was declining in more remote areas. The closure of the Western Cable Company in Valentia meant that the island could no longer field a team.

KERRY, NOW CAPTAINED by one Donie O'Sullivan, reached the National League semi-final but were well beaten by Cavan.

Kerry were expected to dispose of Cork reasonably handily in the Munster final and keep their eyes focused on maroon and white. You can't ever, ever do that with Cork and Kerry paid the price late on.

Cork were in a bit of transition and had drafted six of their under-21 team onto the seniors. Eamonn Young, Dr Jim's brother and an All-Ireland winner in 1945 in his own right, was helping to advise the players on training.

Seamus Mac Gearailt was dismissed and Kerry started to run low on steam as Cork blitzed in goals by Johnny Carroll and Gene McCarthy. Kerry needed a goal themselves, but the man between the posts had no intention of conceding any – Billy Morgan making his debut.

For the first time in nine years, Kerry would not be collecting Munster medals. Cork played better than Galway in the semi-final but two late misses were a let-off for the Tribesman, who went on to beat Meath in the final to claim three in-a-row.

Kerry could only look on with a palpable sense of what might have been.

Cork were in transition in hurling as well, but they had some lovely hurlers coming through. Speculation that Christy Ring might be coming out of retirement (Tipperary's John Doyle had equalled his record haul of eight All-Irelands the year before) proved unfounded, but it turned out that they didn't need the wizard of Cloyne to see off Tipperary in the All-Ireland final, with young captain Gerald McCarthy outstanding.

Nor was there any silverware at county level.

East Kerry reached the county final after a one-point win over West Kerry, but the mighty Mitchels had one last sting in them and won a cracking final by 2-10 to 1-10.

THE 60s WERE a mixed experience for Donie with club and county. But the decade did point him in the direction of the United States. In 1965, he was selected to play in the Cardinal Cushing Games... which proved a fantastic experience as Donie got to know some great players like Christy Ring and Con Paddy O'Sullivan, Bernie Hartigan, Seán Ferris, Red Collier, John Doyle and Jimmy Whan. In 1963, Tom Long, Mick O'Connell and Mick O'Dwyer had been amongst the guest players.

It was an absolutely wonderful trip to the US – one that would stay in Donie's mind and play great significance for him personally very soon, and for his club later on.

In 1965, Donie made his first visit to the United States as part of the Cardinal Cushing Games. Included here are: Front – Fr Jim Aherne, Austin Flynn, Paddy Holden, Christy Ring, Bernie Hartigan, Pat 'Red' Collier, and Tony Whyte. Back – Seán Ferriter, Christy O'Brien, Con P O'Sullivan, Donie, Jimmy Whan, Cathal Flynn and Pat Dunney.

« CHAPTER 9 »

DR JIM BROSNAN was one of the most innovative county chairmen Kerry has ever had. Dr Jim, like his father Con and brother Mick, had worn the Kerry jersey on the sod of Croke Park.

He knew all about Kerry at harvest time in September, but he knew all about planting the roots of football too and his mantra was always about giving players at all ages and grades enough games.

Kerry had to face into the National League in 1967-68 without Johnny Culloty, Seamus Murphy, Mick O'Dwyer, and Mick O'Connell. Though still playing club football, they had enough.

There was an obvious but very unspoken dissatisfaction within the Kerry camp. Kerry's top players were committed to high standards and expected high standards, but it wasn't happening.

Donie O'Sullivan was also absent, but for a different reason.

He had received a scholarship to St John's University in New York to study Educational Psychology – a rare and wonderful opportunity. His old friend Fr Seán Quinlan hadn't forgotten the small boy from the Sem, and his recommendation was crucial.

Donie maintained his training routine while in the college, including practising his distance kicking.

'It was never any kind of innate gift', says Donie matter-of-factly. 'Of course,

I practiced it. To be honest, the US was a brilliant experience. As well as a great educational experience that anyone would appreciate, it was also a great adventure in itself.

'But money was tight, and it could be tough going at times. I appreciated the great support I had over there, but even so it could be lonely at times.'

On his previous, and first visit, to the east coast of the US the previous May, there was some degree of luxury involved. 'It was a great trip. We were staying in a hotel in Manhattan, on Eighth Avenue, and we were taken everywhere.

'We were taken to Washington, and brought into Bobby Kennedy's office... he showed us around the Senate. He was very kind and courteous, and looking back now, I wish that we had had the courage to ask more questions of him.'

Donie's experience during his year in St John's was more basic from day to day. 'Fr Quinlan was from Killarney... and a great footballing man. It was he who suggested I go to America.

'St John's was a big university, and it was an amazing time for me.

'Fr Seán had arranged for me to go out and meet them in the college, and sit for an interview with Dr Sam Fanning, before committing and returning for the year. Sam Fanning was a native of Moneygall in Tipperary, and although he had lived in the US since his youth he was still very much a hurling man.

'I did that interview, and it sounded great.

'And it was!

'But it was a complete change of life. I got free tuition and graduate assistance, but in reality, I was just getting enough to live on. I lived off the campus, in a basement apartment, in an area called Jamaica, which is a neighbourhood in Queens.

'It was a lifetime opportunity, so it was not that difficult to turn my back on football for the year, but when I got out there I have to say it was tougher than I thought it would be.

'I was leaving my comfort zone, living on the bare minimum... but looking back, it was well worth doing, not so much the content of the course itself, but the experience of life.

'I had very few friends out there, though people were pleasant and very helpful to me. But the first few months were quite difficult, as I was straight into a semester and a lot of it was new and alien to me. In the evening time, I usually spent my time catching up on class work, so I didn't get out much.

'In the beginning, I did travel to Gaelic Park when it was possible.

'It was a long journey. I can recall with gratitude Seán O'Shea from Glenflesk and Mike Moriarity of Cloghane coming to Long Island, and ferrying me to Gaelic Park in the Bronx. It was a lesson for me in the importance of the GAA within the Irish diaspora in New York.

'The first time I went, it was such a relief to be back amongst my own, and I did play some games with the Kerry club, but not as much as I would have liked.

'I had a series of muscle injuries, which I blame now on long hours of study, and not eating correctly.

'I found that I got injured too frequently.'

ST JOHN'S WAS not a big basketball college by American standards, and neither was it ever going to attract the cream of American Football scholarships. One thing the college was lacking, however, was an accurate long-distance kicker – a small but key element of their game. Donie wasn't big enough or didn't have a strong enough arm for any traditional route into the game... but kicking?

He never sought it out; that wouldn't have been his way. But some of the St Johns' players were watching this quiet Irishman practicing his craft. The round ball was alien to them, but this lad could kick it.

More out of friendly curiosity than anything else, they asked him to have a go with their own.

Let's face it, kicking is *kicking*.

The oval ball might be a bit different, a bit more demanding in technique, but Donie was more than equal to it. Before long he was kicking with the team. There were no long-term ambitions on anyone's side other than camaraderie.

The New York Jets professional football team were also using the same field as St John's for training.

The Jets were impressed with Donie, both in his skill and his attitude. Just for the fun of it, a casual thing on all sides, they set up an informal kicking competition.

It was a comfortable challenge for Donie.

No pressure, and an art-form that he had been carefully honing for a decade. The New York Jets weren't a rich franchise, as such things went in the American

Football League (it merged with the NFL in 1970 – the champions of the two franchises had played a 'Superbowl' for the first time while Donie was kicking around Shea Stadium in 1966), and manager Herb Weeb Ewbank was used to cutting his cloth to measure.

He set up another bit of a kickaround, keeping his powder dry.

It was good PR on all sides – no harm making a connection to New York's Irish population and cementing a friendship with a prestigious college.

And the chances are that Ewbank was already seeing real possibilities in Donie. This time, they invited a photographer from *Sports Illustrated*.

Ewbank liked what he saw.

Actually, he liked it an awful lot.

Herb needed a top-quality kicker, and he had just found one.

To say that Donie was tempted is a big understatement. Anyone would be – the glamour came with real money and the Jets were a coming team. He came very close to signing. But… well, Donie wasn't a man swayed by such lures; he always walked a straight road rather than an easy one.

And although he liked his prospective teammates and enjoyed the game, it was not something that called to his soul. If the offer had come from the club at the end of 1966, perhaps he would have given it some consideration, but the Jets did not make a formal approach until February 1967.

'I was settled in by the following February, and more confident, and also more aware of the downside of life as a kicker on an American Football team.

'Even at that stage, I thought Ireland was a better country to grow old in, and I missed playing with Kerry and the lads. In American Football, the kicker plays more of a side role, coming on as a specialist rather than being part of the team.

'I knew so little about it really, and wearing that helmet and all of that gear that they wear… I felt like a spaceman. Their kickers weren't paid that much either, they were a bit like the 'hired help' on the team, it seemed to me.

'Actually, kicking was probably the last role you would like to have on a team out there. I was able to manage the ball, no problem… I could kick it.

'I often feel that there's someone guiding you through life and that home was where I was meant to be.'

The Jets won the AFL Championship in 1968.

A year later, they shocked everyone by beating the NFL Champions the

Baltimore Colts in the Superbowl (it was the third such final, but the first to attract the moniker. They were 19.5 point underdogs and the first AFL team to win the final. Joe Namath was MVP and kicker Jim Turner had three field goals in the 16-7 victory).

Regrets?

'None, and that tells me that I made the right decision', smiles Donie.

He got injured soon after turning down Ewbank, an injury that he struggled with for several months. He enjoyed his time in New York, but one year was enough.

Home was calling, and so was the Kerry team.

IT WAS THE only Munster Championship that Donie missed in his playing days, and if you had to miss one, 1967 was the right one. Missing so many icons of the game, Kerry were blooding a lot of younger players.

They got past Limerick comfortably enough, but everyone knew that the real test would be Cork.

There was a bite between the two sides in the Munster final, right from the throw-in and the tone never improved from there. Cork retained their Munster title by a single, solitary point after Kerry had hauled back a five-point gap, having disappointed in the first-half.

Kerry's football was okay, but their shooting was very poor.

A rapid improvement saw Kerry get to within one point, despite Billy Morgan making a brilliant full-length save to deny DJ Crowley what looked like a certain goal. Cork had beaten Kerry in the championship back-to-back for the first time in their history.

Galway, probably fatigued after the National League final in New York, went down surprisingly tamely to Mayo. Cork and Meath fought out the All-Ireland final, with Meath recovering from a 0-3 to 0-1 deficit to sneak it with a fisted goal by Terry Kearns.

RUMBLINGS IN NORTHERN Ireland were growing louder through the decade, with civil rights for the Catholic minority a huge issue, and, in all fairness, with very good reason.

The likes of MP Austin Currie were creditably highlighting the issue. On October 5, 1968, a peaceful protest march began. A similar march, though officially banned, had already passed off without incident.

This one didn't.

The unionist government was clearly determined to shut it down, relying on the raw brute force of the RUC to do so. That wasn't exactly uncommon at protests world-wide during the 60s, an age where rising confidence in themselves saw young people especially challenge the older generation.

What the RUC or the authorities had failed to comprehend was the reason why such actions now came with a price tag. RTÉ cameraman Gay O'Brien was there, covering it like any ordinary news story, but he kept his camera rolling. The footage went all around the world.

The British government tried their usual bluff and bluster, but for the Irish diaspora around the world, especially in the US, their credibility was shattered. Northern Ireland wasn't quite at war, not yet, but it was now on a war footing along clearly delineated lines and the Battle of the Bogside was already an inevitability.

In Croke Park, Kerry found themselves at a crossroads.

They were walloped by Down in the Cuchulainn Tournament final. Dr Jim Brosnan knew full well that things were at a low ebb in Kerry football. Kerry had already been beaten by Cork in the National League.

Jackie Lyne had guided Legion to the O'Donoghue Cup in 1967 and he was appointed Kerry trainer in early 1968 – I think it's fair to surmise that the respect he was held in by the Kerry footballers, not least the recent retirees, was a factor. O'Dwyer and O'Connell had been outstanding in Waterville's 1967 triumphs in the South Kerry Championship, Kerry Junior Championship, and Urban League.

A challenge game was held.

Kerry 'Past' versus Kerry 'Present'.

The 'Past' won the game, with O'Connell and Seamus Murphy imperious in general play; it wasn't hard for Dr Jim to persuade them to come back for the county. Beaufort teenage sensation Brendan Lynch was slotting in comfortably into the team.

The team that faced Cork that July was a very different one to the side that lost in the league in January.

Cork had a great debutante of their own – Ray Cummins scoring a cracking goal. Donal Hunt added another. They were seven points in front early on, but O'Connell thrived in such circumstances and he rose to new heights, both literally and figuratively. O'Connell, Brendan Lynch and Pat Griffin kicked 0-4 apiece, Eamonn O'Donoghue had 1-1, slotting a goal. Kerry went through by 1-21 to 3-8.

Kerry were still concerned about their goalkeeping position, however. On the Monday night before the All-Ireland semi-final, Jackie Lyne and county board secretary Tadhg Crowley left the meeting in the Park Place Hotel at the top of High Street in Killarney and made their way up to Sunny Hill, near the Parish Hall, to knock on Johnny Culloty's door.

Culloty duly trained with the team for one night before lining out in the All-Ireland semi-final. He was still young, and as fit and capable as ever.

Longford had stunned everybody by winning out Leinster in 1968. They had met the big guns Dublin, Meath and Laois, and weren't intimidated at facing the green and gold either.

Kerry had goals from Pat Griffin (who finished with 1-4) and Dom O'Donnell for a 2-6 to 0-7 half-time lead. Longford actually led with 10 minutes to go, with goals from Tom Mulvihill and a Jackie Devine penalty. It could have been more, but Culloty repaid all trust in him with a superb save that denied the dangerous Devine a second goal.

Kerry used all their guile to come through 2-13 to 2-11.

Down and Seán O'Neill saw off Galway and carried their hoodoo over Kerry into Croke Park. Seán O'Neill and John Murphy blasted home early goals for a 2-3 to 0-1 lead after eight minutes that had Kerry always chasing the game.

They led by 2-7 to 0-5 at half-time.

Kerry were vastly improved in the second-half, but a very late goal from Brendan Lynch, direct from a free, wasn't enough to save Kerry. 2-12 to 1-13. So near... and still so far away.

'We had many players back on the team,' notes Donie. 'But we sorely missed Tom Long in 1968... he would have made all the difference in the final, in my opinion.'

NOBODY WAS TALKING about Spa as the newcomers in East Kerry anymore; they were an established powerhouse. A convincing victory in the Rathmore Carnival Tournament rubber-stamped that (with no senior county league, such tournaments were both common and necessary for club players to get games). During a debate on raising players' travelling expenses (don't get excited about pay for play – it was raised from a pittance to a slightly bigger pittance) Donie was singled out for travelling from Dublin on three separate occasions and bringing players with him, while Tim Sheehan from Kilcummin was also mentioned for coming from Cork on six separate trips.

Both players had played in a cracking East Kerry League match that year, in which Spa had led by five points in the dying minutes only for Kilcummin to switch Dan Dwyer from defence to attack. It was a master-stroke as Dan engineered two goals for the win.

But it was Crokes who were the undisputed kingpins of East Kerry. They had won nine titles in 12 years. Crokes, quite simply, were and are the team to beat. And they had one of their greatest teams ever in 1968... Con O'Meara, Paddy 'Bomber' O'Shea, Donal 'Socky' Lynch, Gerard Cullinane, Con Clifford, Fergus Moroney, Jackie Looney, Tom Long (the former Gaeltacht and Kerry star), Dan Kelliher, Tom Looney... Spa knew the mountain they had to climb in the final.

One of Crokes' big stars, Eamonn Fitzgerald, travelled down with Donie and Mick Gleeson – he had won a Dublin championship with Erin's Hope. The three stopped in Brennan's Glen to stretch their legs for a few minutes.

The match throw-in was delayed by a few minutes and none of the three got much of a warm-up besides that brief stop!

Spa were good, but Crokes were seasoned veterans with incredible teamwork. In the end, they had too much for Spa, even with Donie playing at his best. And I do mean his absolute best – Donie covered every inch of the ground.

Spa actually led early on, with Mick Gleeson shading a fantastic duel with his travelling companion and future Kerry teammate Eamonn Fitzgerald (whose nephew Fionn would later follow him into a county geansaí). However, in the 18th minute, Tom Long launched a rasper that young Spa keeper Jackie Foley just managed to bat away... only for Con Clifford to fist home the rebound.

Straight from the kickout, Long grabbed the ball and blasted another one to the net and quickly added a point. Crokes led by 2-1 to 0-5 at half-time despite having been outplayed for most of the half.

Again, Spa reeled off early points in the second-half, only to see Long burst through to send a bullet to the net, and then win a penalty converted by Clifford. Spa stayed in touch with some good scores, but Patsy O'Connor and Fergus

Moroney sealed it.

Crokes had 10 wins since 1956, with the '61 captain Jackie Looney having a part in each victory.

It had taken 13 years to amass those titles.

Incredibly, Crokes wouldn't win one again for another 13 years.

SADLY, JIMMY LUCEY of Caragh Lake, so recently a Kerry teammate of Donie's along with his brothers, passed away in February, 1969, after a long illness. Jimmy was just 28 years old.

East Kerry were reigning champions, and Dr Crokes were champions of the District, so they had the right to nominate the captain. The problem was that Dr Crokes didn't have a player on the county panel at the time. The club debated the matter.

There was only two realistic candidates.

Donie O'Sullivan had played with Dr Crokes before Spa had a team and helped them to win titles. Johnny Culloty, hugely popular among the Crokes club (Johnny was and is popular everywhere), was a stalwart of their greatest rivals, Killarney Legion.

In the end, the fact that Donie had captained Kerry in 1966, whereas Johnny had never captained the county team, was the decisive factor.

It was a bit of a strange decision in retrospect, but it didn't bother Donie in the slightest. He was more than happy to follow his close friend and teammate onto the field.

The issue of the captaincy is a regular bone of contention in Kerry, where the county champions get the honour of nominating the captain. Some people argue that the system is out of date and that most counties select their captain on experience and merit. All I can say is that it usually arises in conversation… only after Kerry lose.

Kerry had a great National League.

Kerry won six games, including beating Cork twice (two good games), and drew just one game (with Mayo) on the way to the 'Home' final against Offaly. They beat them well, 3-11 to 0-8. That was a good Offaly team, and Kerry would meet them again!

That win saw Kerry play in the league final over in Gaelic Park in New York.

New York had a very good side at the time, with Jimmy Foley of Keel and Mick Moynihan of Rathmore lining out with Tom Furlong of Offaly in the forwards. It was a brilliant game, nip and tuck all through.

Kerry lost Mick O'Connell to injury but replacement Pat Moynihan of Gneeveguilla was superb in the middle. Kerry trailed by 2-2 to 0-4 at the break and New York led by three late on, only for O'Connell to give a marvellous kicking display to level.

Near the finish, Mick O'Dwyer fisted over to give Kerry the lead, but Tom Furlong won and converted a free to level things.

The final was played over two legs, on successive Sundays, and a week later John Kerry O'Donnell's Gaelic Park was again breathing heavily with anticipation.

Two early goals by Des Ryan had Kerry in trouble but they managed to battle back, O'Connell with a late point putting it into extra-time. Kerry then scored a whopping 1-9 on the trot as fatigue caught the New Yorkers – Derry Crowley scored the goal and Brendan Lynch hit another one late on to seal a 2-21 to 2-12 victory.

Kerry: Johnny Culloty; Seamus Murphy, Paud O'Donoghue, Seamus Mac Gearailt; Donie O'Sullivan, Mick Morris, Micheal Ó Sé; Mick Fleming, DJ Crowley; Brendan Lynch, Christy O'Sullivan, Eamonn O'Donoghue; Tom Prendergast, Liam Higgins, Mick O'Dwyer. Subs Mick O'Connell, Derry Crowley.

WATERFORD GOT AN early goal, but a strong second quarter saw Kerry lead by 1-11 to 1-4. Once again Waterford reeled them in, and once again Kerry had the fitness to win the fourth quarter by 0-5 to 0-1 for a comfortable 1-18 to 2-7 victory.

A week later, Jack Lynch led Fianna Fail to victory in his first campaign as leader. John O'Leary had topped the South Kerry poll, with Fianna Fail colleague Timothy 'Chub' O'Connor second. Fine Gael's Michael Begley had passed out his running mate Patrick O'Connor Scarteen to take the third seat.

The Munster final was a different proposition to Waterford. Cork were dangerous.

Billy Morgan, young Brian Murphy, Frank Cogan, Denis Coughlan, Millstreet's Denny Long, John Crowley and the big dual full-forward Ray Cummins… these were known men, and they had Teddy Holland on the bench.

Kerry led by 0-4 to 0-1, but Cork got two penalties. Denis Coughlan hit the left upright and Seamus Fitzgerald dived on it to prevent a rebound.

He had touched it on the ground... another penalty.

Johnny Culloty caught Donal Hunt's shot and cleared it. At half-time it was just 0-5 to 0-4, but Kerry added five points on the trot to their lead in the third quarter. Mick O'Connell scored the best point of the lot.

He split the posts from all of 60 yards, no exaggeration, only for the referee to call it back. So, O'Connell put the ball down again... and wordlessly repeated the feat.

He never glanced at the referee, why would he? Billy Morgan made a brilliant save to deny Liam Higgins late on. Flor Hayes' late goal was little consolation for the disconsolate rebels.

By the time the Kerry team were arriving back in Killarney from Cork's Athletic Grounds, Apollo 11 was nearing its lunar destination and Neil Armstrong was about to take a small step for a man and a giant leap for mankind...

Cavan surprised All-Ireland champions Down in the Ulster final a week later. The championship had just been blown wide open, and Kerry knew it.

SEMI-FINAL. KERRY Vs MAYO.

You'd have to love Mayo – Kerry have beaten them in almost every meeting for 60 years when the chips were down, but they have always given as good as they got and came back for more. The 1969 All-Ireland semi-final was arguably the best game of all between the two teams.

A brace from Joe Corcoran had Mayo 0-4 to 0-3 ahead before Liam Higgins rattled the crossbar. O'Connell and O'Dwyer frees got it back to 0-5 apiece. Kerry were on top now, O'Dwyer and Pat Griffin putting them in front. Mick Gleeson hit the post and had a shot blocked on the line.

Nerveless Joe Corcoran kicked two frees to make it 0-7 apiece at half-time. He hit another two minutes after the break, but Kerry swarmed in front through O'Dwyer (two), Pat Griffin, O'Connell, Mick Gleeson, teenager Brendan Lynch and Eamonn O'Donoghue. Mayo weren't done, though – PJ Loftus lofted a ball over the Kerry defence and Des Griffin latched onto it, giving Johnny Culloty no chance. Kerry had three wides in-a-row before Joe Corcoran pointed to cut the gap to one.

A great run by Willie McGee was ended illegally and Mayo had a free with one minute left on the clock. Joe Corcoran had split the posts five times but, inexplicably, it was Seamus O'Dowd who took it... and the ball curled wide.

0-14 to 1-10, and Kerry had just about scraped through.

Offaly awaited in the final… a great Offaly side.

Young Martin Furlong in goal. Big Paddy McCormack, whom Micheal O'Hehir had christened 'The Iron Man from Rhode' outside him. It was said that if McCormack was out injured, you could just stick a photograph of him on the crossbar and it would put the full-forward off – that was the kind of presence he had. *Butch Cassidy and the Sundance Kid* were doing their gallivanting in cinemas at the time – neither of them would have tried their antics on big Paddy! Willie Bryan was in midfield, nigh on as household a name as O'Connell himself. Tony McTeague and Seán Evans in the forwards.

THERE WAS MAJOR surprise when the Kerry team was picked for the final. Donie O'Sullivan, who had played superbly all along, was dropped… and no one knew why. Including Donie.

He had been replaced by Mick Fleming after picking up a knock in the semi-final, but wasn't injured and was doing fine in training. To this day, he doesn't know why he was omitted – and if politics was involved, as most people suspected, he isn't going to say.

The 'Charity of Silence' is a phrase that is close to Donie's heart, and it is one he has applied when repeatedly questioned over the last 50 years about his demotion from the Kerry team before the 1969 All-Ireland final.

He repeats it now.

'Things like that are a part of life, really,' he sums up.

'Maybe the seminary discipline helped me too, I don't know. I heard the team announced on a radio, but there was no point in getting angry or even thinking of walking away…' and then he stops himself.

'The Charity of Silence!'

There were doubts about O'Connell's fitness.

He was the last player to emerge from the Kerry dressing-room and was greeted by a huge cheer. Mick Gleeson opened the scoring in the atrocious weather and he, Brendan Lynch, and Liam Higgins helped Kerry into a 0-4 to 0-2 lead. Offaly almost got in on goal twice – Mick Morris made a brilliant block, and Johnny Culloty made a fine save.

DJ Crowley pointed from long range to leave Kerry ahead by 0-5 to 0-2 at the break – surely not enough against that massive wind? In fact, Offaly were almost on level terms straightaway – if Johnny Culloty's first half save was good, his second one against Seán Evans was simply magical.

Culloty had studied and prepared for Evans' quick shooting style – it was as much about preparation as instinct, Johnny never lacked for either.

Two Offaly points had the gap down to one, but Mick O'Dwyer and DJ Crowley restored it. Tom Prendergast at wing back was flying. Once again, Offaly cut it back to 0-7 to 0-6, but DJ Crowley in particular led Kerry in a battling fourth quarter that saw them win a tough battle by 0-10 to 0-7.

SPA SAW OFF Kilcummin in the O'Donoghue Cup quarter-final in August, and Killarney Legion in the semi-final. On the other side, Dr Crokes needed two late goals to see off the challenge of a great Rathmore side.

Spa were a young team for the most part. Crokes, though still unquestionably great, couldn't match Spa's speed. They were always the better side, but had to keep proving it. Donie stepped up to take a first-half penalty and struck it well, but Crokes' keeper Con O'Meara made a great save, though at the expense of a '50' which was duly pointed, giving Spa an important psychological boost.

Spa led by 0-9 to 0-3 at half-time, with Connie Doolan's shooting radar unerring, and the writing was clearly on the wall.

Cormac Moroney, in particular, battled hard to get Crokes back into it in the second-half in a pulsating battle, but Spa's county players, Donie, Mick and Pat Casey were magnificent. With two minutes left and four points between them, it looked safely in the bag, but Spa got one last fright when a late attempt at goal by Crokes crashed back off the upright. The final whistle saw scenes of relief as much as jubilation as Mick Gleeson lifted the cup.

The Spa team was: Jackie Foley; Denny Doolan, Brian Fenton, Jim Gleeson; Johnny Batt Cronin, Jack Morris, Donie O'Sullivan; Pat Casey, John O'Sullivan; Barry O'Connor, Mick Myers, Michael O'Donoghue; Connie Doolan, Mick Gleeson, Johnny Doolan.

'Beating Crokes in a final was a huge statement for Spa.

'It's a compliment to Crokes to say that they were the benchmark for football in East Kerry at the time. Once that team had beaten Crokes in an O'Donoghue final, we felt confident in ourselves facing anyone.

'It was that game more than any other that made that Spa team', according to Donie. 'We learned a good deal from our defeat the previous year.

'Lessons learned from losing are many… and should be lessons for life.'

IT WAS AN interesting county championship.

East Kerry faced Mitchels in the semi-final. This was the last throw of the dice from one of the greatest teams in Kerry's county championship history.

They gave East Kerry a huge fright – Weeshie Fogarty had to make two great saves to deny 'Thorny' O'Shea goals. Waterville, meanwhile, had seen off Mid Kerry despite the absence of Mick O'Connell.

East Kerry was facing a much tougher game to win than their previous final success – lashing rain and a heavy ground was a huge test of skill; both sides passed with flying colours. Donie marked Mick O'Dwyer, both men directing operations for their respective teams as well. Donal Kavanagh gave East Kerry the fillip of an early goal for a 1-5 to 0-3 half-time lead, but Mick O'Neill goaled in turn.

In the end it was 2-7 to 1-8.

To make it better, Killarney's hurling team went a step further than the previous year, beating Stacks (as Mitchels didn't have a hurling team, Mitchels stalwarts like Niall Sheehy and Seamus Roche played in black and amber) to win their only county hurling championship.

Con O'Meara captained the Killarney team and a large number of dual players featured, including the likes of the Culloty brothers, Dan Kelliher, Derry Crowley, Tom Prendergast, and Mick Spillane.

Long delays in fixtures meant that the Munster Club Championship was never completed.

With East Kerry once again having the choice of nominating the captain and Spa the O'Donoghue Cup champions, there was never any doubt about who would be wearing the armband the next time that Kerry took the field.

Donie would return to the US again and again, and lecture in San Diego for two decades, but his first real taste of the American experience was when he spent a year studying at St John's in 1966-67 when his kicking with the college American Football team brought him to the attention of the New York Jets.

Donie and teammates photographed on their 'World Tour' with Kerry in the spring of 1969. Many years later Donie and Johnny Culloty would make a presentation to former Kerry County Board chairman, Dr Jim Brosnan as a thank you for his brilliant work in making that tour happen.

« CHAPTER 10 »

From quiet homes and first beginning
Out to the undiscovered ends
There's nothing worth the wear of winning
But laughter and the love of friends

– Hilaire Belloc

A NEW DECADE.

The 'Swinging Sixties' were at an end.

Welcome to the 70s.

Already it was clear that it was going to be a bleak one for Northern Ireland – the infamous 'Battle of the Bogside' in Derry the previous August made that obvious. In fact, there was strong pressure on the government to support the nationalist population of the Six Counties of Northern Ireland and that would have consequences of its own.

Life changed dramatically in the late-60s and early-70s. The prevalence of television, in particular, was a medium that, although subject to state control, had a very wide latitude in reporting on and to society. Although farming was still by far the biggest occupation, there were more jobs in tourism, industry, and especially the expansion of state bodies. Increasing affluence combined with an increase in investment in education resulted in a young educated people.

Those young people had a better chance of growing up in their native country than practically any Irish generation for the past two centuries. Emigration was still relatively common, but nothing like the mass exodus of previous years. Moreover, young people didn't have to put in the same back-breaking hours as their forefathers for a living, as machinery increasingly took the place of manual labour in many jobs.

More and more of them lived near each other, as well. Irish society was becoming increasingly urbanised.

The late 60s had seen a building boom. People who were building their own home could avail of a £310 government grant, another means-tested £300 grant from Kerry County Council, and get a council loan at a relatively cheap rate to build their house. Consider that Ireland's average weekly wage was around £20, and you can see how the first rung of the property ladder was actually within reach.

The housing estates of Ardshanavooley, Park Rd., and Pinewood were all built in those years. Not only that, but those houses proved to be good value. During the 70s, wages doubled to almost £40 a week by 1973, £68 a week in '76, and over £100 a week by the end of the decade.

As more and more people possessed cars and had a sufficiency of indoor entertainment – again, television played a huge role – people became more sedentary.

Clothing was cheaper to purchase, and advertising encouraged rapid fashion change at affordable prices. Penneys, that staple of Irish retail, had started selling big quantities of cheap and cheerful clothing lines in 1969 when Arthur Ryan, who had worked for Ben Dunne Snr., applied the same technique to clothing. It was an almost instant phenomenon.

If you grew up in Ireland at any time after that, you probably grew up wearing Penney's clothing.

The consumption of alcohol has always been a problem in Ireland. Unfortunately, for too many people, especially young people, new-found confidence and prosperity, plus a rejection of traditional values, carried a veneer of hedonism in too many cases. The number of special exemption orders granted by the courts – to allow drink to be served outside normal licensing hours –

increased from 6,342 in 1967 to 14,814 in '72, and would more than double in the following five years again.

Patrick McDonnell, chairman of the National Off Licence Traders Association, wrote to the government to complain that the Minister for Justice Des O'Malley 'is not taking any notice of the serious problem of teenagers consuming alcoholic drinks. The situation is ready to erupt into a national scandal and will, if not erased now, have disastrous effects on the physical, mental and moral conditions of the children of Ireland'.

Jack Lynch publicly reprimanded McDonnell for what he felt was the unsuitable tone of the message. He might have been better off giving consideration to its substance.

THINGS WERE CHANGING on the football field, too, with provincial finals and All-Ireland semi-finals and finals extended to 80 minutes.

The theory was that soccer was 90 minutes and rugby was 80, so GAA supporters were feeling a bit short-changed. What wasn't considered, understandably enough, is that gaelic games are far less stop/start and the ball moves around the field much faster.

Many reasons have been offered for the increase in professional standards and demands in gaelic games, but the increased fitness demanded to last that long was very much a prime mover and the counties that were quickest to realise it – and have the resources to back it up – succeeded.

Donie was in midfield beside DJ Crowley for most of the National League. beating Galway by 3-9 to 0-10 on March 1. It was Kerry and Mayo in the league semi-final, and this time a goal from Liam Higgins wasn't enough to stop Mayo who later claimed the title, beating Down in the final.

It wasn't the most auspicious start to a new season, but the Kerry team had already been 'flying high' before their bumpy ending to the league – having headed Down Under on the trip of a lifetime.

THAT TRIP HAD been planned for a while.

Harry Beitzel, a famous referee and commentator on Australian Rules football, had happened to see a broadcast of a few of the All-Ireland finals. He saw similarities with his own game and, well aware of the influence of the big Irish diaspora in Australia, started arranging for an Aussie Rules team to tour Ireland. Although neither the Australian VFL or Irish GAA were willing to invest in the project, the players loved the idea and the 'Galahs' duly arrived in Ireland.

It didn't generate much excitement beforehand – only 20,000 turned up – but that changed when the Australians, playing a game new to most of them, destroyed both Meath and Mayo. They flew to New York and lost to the New York football team in a game marred by some violence – Australian captain Ron Barrassi had his nose broken.

Their trip didn't make the profit that Beitzel was hoping for, but a precedent was established. Some months later, Meath became the first Irish team to tour Australia.

Kerry, who had been among the first Irish counties to tour the US in 1926, were eager to follow suit.

Kerry started arranging a trip for the 1969 All-Ireland champions (Central Council had already refused to sanction an earlier trip; they couldn't do so a second time).

Australia was the main destination, but they actually took in Amsterdam, Singapore, Auckland, New Zealand, Fiji... and San Francisco, Chicago, and New York along the way!

Twenty-one players travelled – Mick Fleming was studying in England and Mick O'Connell was unavailable. Amongst the travelling party were Paddy O'Donoghue, founder and proprietor of the Gleneagle Hotel since 1957, Willie Lanigan who had a shop on Henn St in Killarney (now Plunkett St), and New St publican Charlie Foley (he was a Kerry selector in the 1930s and had travelled to the States with the Kerry team).

'It took huge funding, and Dr Jim Brosnan was the driving force behind it,' explains Donie. 'The planes we were travelling on weren't fuelled for long distance, so there were many stops, and places to see.

'It's always a good excuse to stop in Honolulu for gasoline!

'It was a fabulous trip for us all.

'We stayed in the best hotels, and we trained while we were there. We knew that we were coming home and going straight into a championship. We didn't feel it was risky going at that time of the year.

'An unforgettable experience, and the weather was superb, but we looked after ourselves at the same time while we were out there.

'There was not much drinking done on that trip. There was very little drinking done by that group while we were home, so nobody did much drinking out there either.

'It was the same with most other teams… there was a maturity and self-discipline amongst that group of players. A lot of teams at that time might have only one or two lads who even took a drink.'

THE CELTIC CLUB in Perth put on a great welcome for their Kerry visitors. Kerry played a game at the Subiacon Oval and watched an Aussie Rules match – very impressed by the fitness levels of the professionals.

They went from Perth to Adelaide, where they agreed to play a challenge game against an AFL side, the first-half using an oval ball and the second-half a gaelic football. It was 2-2 to 1-5 at half-time and Dr Jim Brosnan agreed to stay with the oval ball as the game was so exciting.

Donie, for one, was loving the challenge, as was Tom Prendergast. Kerry won well in the finish, 7-13 to 3-5. After the match, Adelaide captain Peter Darley described Prendergast as 'the greatest small man I have ever seen, his display was superb'.

Tom was one of the all-time greats (and still an officer of his beloved Keel GAA club to this day) and 1970 was his greatest year; he was simply untouchable.

In Melbourne, they played at the famous MCG. Then it was on to Wagga Wagga ('Australian aborigines didn't have plurals in their language', explains Donie, who was fascinated by the complexities of their culture) to play a local team who were generous hosts. All the Kerry players loved the friendliness and open approach that is endemic of the Australian national character.

The places were fascinating, but it's the memories of the friendships that made it such a wonderful holiday. Donie and Gneeveguilla's Pat Moynihan stayed with Max Kincade. It was a very enjoyable visit – so much so that they overslept and missed their morning flight.

While John D Hickey of the *Irish Independent* was reporting on their disappearance, Max was arranging for the pair to take a later flight on a small plane to Sydney, where they celebrated St Patrick's Day.

After that, it was Fiji and on to San Francisco, where Donie met with Fr

Gerry Murphy, one of the Gabha Murphys of Barradubh ('gabha' simply means blacksmith, the family's original trade). Names like Moynihan, O'Sullivan, Fleming, Murphy, and O'Donoghue are so commonplace around Killarney that they are often distinguished by sobriquet.

In Nevada they stayed at the Shamrock Inn, owned by the Brosnans from Currow. Chicago next... and lastly Donie's old hunting ground of New York, before jetting back to Ireland.

It was the trip of a lifetime.

It also whetted their appetites. It happened because of football and they would pay it back in the same currency.

Back home, and with a championship to defend, Seamus Mac Gearailt was a major absentee, having suffered a knee injury. Pat Griffin was able to play but starting to struggle with a back injury he had picked up in that fairly rough game in Wagga Wagga.

As All-Ireland champions, Kerry weren't in any hurry to freshen up their senior panel – John O'Keeffe of Austin Stacks, All-Ireland winner Frank's son, was an exception.

KERRY LED BY seven points in the opening 10 minutes of the first round in Munster. Limerick rallied well with a goal from Pat Murphy after Eamonn Cregan's free hit the upright.

Kerry responded with seven points on the trot to make it 0-15 to 1-3 at half-time. Mick Gleeson goaled on the restart but Seán Burke reacted fastest after Johnny Culloty saved Cregan's penalty and tapped the rebound home.

Pat Griffin set up Mick Gleeson for his second goal to seal a 2-19 to 2-5 victory. Cork were up next.

Cork had won the last three minor All-Irelands and had a young and hungry team. They had a few lessons yet to learn, though. Pat Griffin exchanged passes with Liam Higgins before slotting a goal. Mick O'Dwyer and Pat added points, before Griffin turned provider, Higgins blasting past Billy Morgan.

Mick O'Connell kicked four points in-a-row. It was 2-12 to 0-4 by half-time; there was only going to be one winner here!

In fairness to Cork, they did put up a great second-half battle. Bernie O'Neill tried hard at midfield and Denis Coughlan was at his brilliant best with 2-4, but

Kerry had too much in hand. Donie O'Sullivan, the first Spa man to play for Kerry, lifted the Munster cup.

It was Derry in the All-Ireland semi-final.

This was a young Derry side for the most part, with Seán O'Connell leading them on the field. Kerry were in trouble early on with O'Connell hobbling off to be treated by masseur and *Kerryman* reporter Owen McCrohan, after a collision with Seamus Lagan.

By the time he returned in the 16th minute, Kerry were down 0-5 to 0-1 and in disarray.

It could have been worse.

Brendan Lynch pulled a point back, but Derry had a chance to go clear when Seán O'Connell stepped up to a penalty. Johnny Culloty read it well and saved – it lifted Kerry and deflated Derry. At half-time Derry were in front, but the gap was a manageable 0-8 to 0-6.

The lead was down to a single point when Seán O'Connell won Derry's second penalty. This time it was Seamus Lagan who stepped up, but the ball flashed wide of the post.

Donie remembers the game well.

'In 1970 we got a lot of breaks, especially against Derry. They were the team that we were most worried about that year. Ten minutes after half-time when they were leading, they missed their second penalty.

'If they had scored either of those, I doubt if we would have won it. But that was the breaking point.'

Kerry went in front and never looked back.

They had to survive one more scare, Seamus Murphy clearing from Seán O'Connell, but Kerry went on to win by 0-23 to 0-10. To say that the scoreline doesn't reflect the game is a huge under-statement!

'That scoreline tells you little about that game!' Donie stresses.

MEATH HAD EDGED out the game of the year so far, beating Offaly in the Leinster final by 2-22 to 5-12.

Meath were a coming team. Harry Beitzel's Australian team visit in 1967 was just one of the coaching and tactical innovations they were taking on board. Gormanston was the first place in the country to host regular coaching courses.

The Kerry minors had beaten Cork to win Munster with a team that included Mickey Ned O'Sullivan, John Egan, Jimmy Deenihan, Ger O'Keeffe and Ger Power. They would have to wait for their All-Irelands, though; Galway had the upper hand in the minor final.

Aodh Ó Ruairc called the teams out over the tannoy as the senior teams took the field – the teacher and principal of St Colmcille's carried out the role for many years and spoke with the same confidence as he did in his day job to a smaller, younger, but no doubt equally enthralled audience (the Oireachtas Award for writing drama for Primary Schools is named after him).

There were cheers but no great furore as the names were called out – this was long before the modern practice of naming false teams to disguise team strategies until the last moment.

THE ALL-IRELAND FINAL was a close game, and a good game.

It was point-for-point in the first quarter. Eamonn O'Donoghue had a goal chance well saved. It was 0-6 apiece when Mick O'Dwyer and Brendan Lynch opened up a two-point lead for the first time.

Kerry hit the crossbar.

Mickey Fay, himself a contender for Footballer of the Year, kicked the last point of the first-half.

The scoreboard had Kerry 0-9, Meath 0-8.

There was a long way to go.

Kerry's captain wasn't going any further, however.

Donie had been playing very well but a pulled muscle in the 15th minute was the beginning of the end of his All-Ireland final. He played on until the 35th minute.

After that, all he could do was watch as destiny unfolded.

'The whole back of my leg muscle was torn,' he remembers. 'It was a fairly bad injury, but, of course, I played on for as long as I could.' His hamstring was badly torn, however.

'I have no idea how exactly it happened, but... whatever way I ran forward, it just went. I knew I had to go off.' All these years later, Donie presents his injury so early in the game as just one of 'life's knocks'.

'A reminder of how fragile we all are in reality!

'It would have been worse, much worse… if we had lost. I was able to go up the Hogan Stand and receive the cup, which can be an ordeal in itself, but a huge honour, and a humbling one.'

Donie O'Sullivan had the Sam Maguire Cup to raise… but before that!

'All the dignitaries were there… and of course President Eamonn De Valera, and we had a brief conversation in Irish, which I appreciate now.'

In the second-half, Kerry had kicked four points in-a-row through Mick O'Dwyer, Mick Gleeson, Eamonn O'Donoghue and Brendan Lynch… to go in front 0-14 to 0-9. No give in the slightest by Meath; back came Fay with two points. Pat Griffin pointed for Kerry. Mick Gleeson had come out to the half-forward line now and was hugely effective.

Mick O'Dwyer lobbed the ball into the Meath goalmouth. DJ Crowley and Jack Quinn contested it. McCormack managed to knock it away, but Mick Gleeson pounced like a hawk and volleyed it left-legged into the net.

It was an opportunistic goal, but a brilliant one.

With 20 minutes left and bodies feeling the strain by now, Kerry were ahead by 1-17 to 0-12. In later years Meath would become famous for their sheer dogged refusal to ever accept their fate tamely – that's not a trait that they licked up from the stones.

This Meath team had absolutely no give in them either.

Five points on the trot brought them right back into it. Mick O'Connell made it 1-18 to 0-17, but Meath cancelled that.

A one score game.

DJ Crowley had had enough of it, slicing straight through the Meath defence. DJ soloed past two despairing Meath men before burying an absolute rocket of a shot past a hapless Seán McCormack with his right.

It remains to this day one of the most famous goals ever scored in Croke Park.

JUST A WEEK later, East Kerry faced Waterville for the third year in-a-row in the county final, having already seen off West Kerry, Shannon Rangers and Mid Kerry.

Trained by Donie Sheehan, East Kerry were that small bit better, winning 1-15 to 0-15. Small margins. Waterville, supplemented by Mick O'Connell, Mick O'Neill, Seán O'Shea and Mick Leary were equal to the very best in the county, and were far more than a village team.

The O'Donoghue Cup produced a big shock. Reigning champions Spa were favourites against Listry. The biggest problem was that Listry didn't care – they gave every bit as good as they got and in the finish they were the East Kerry champions for the first (and so far, last) time. Pa Joe Sweeney and Pat Healy were indomitable in midfield against Pat Casey and John Cahill. Phil Scully in goal defied all of Spa's best efforts.

THE GAA HAD initially spread rapidly after its foundation in 1884, but it had started to struggle very rapidly as athletics continued their close affiliations with English competitions, and rugby and cricket re-asserted themselves.

In fact, the GAA in Kerry and everywhere else struggled to survive. One of the important mainstays that helped it onto a more stable footing was the ban on members playing 'foreign' sports. Although unstated, it was tacitly understood from early on that 'foreign' only referred to those sports that could be seen as an alternative or even a threat to the GAA.

In 1938, the GAA suffered a big public backlash when they criticised recently inaugurated President Douglas Hyde for attending an Ireland v Poland soccer match and removed him as a Patron of the association. Hyde was not just a gaelic scholar, he was a founding member and first president of the Gaelic League.

Oscar Traynor was the OC for Dublin IRA on the anti-treaty side in the Civil War. He was elected to the Dáil in 1932 and held his seat for three decades. He was Minister for Defence during 'The Emergency'. He was a staunch republican all his life.

He was also a former professional soccer player with Glasgow Celtic and became president of the FAI in 1948.

The GAA put a bold face on it in public, but a hard lesson had been learned. Nonetheless, the Ban was staying. The idealism of the GAA representing a national culture rather than mere sports married perfectly with the pragmatism of maintaining an exclusive sporting dominance. A motion at the 1939 Congress to reinstate Hyde was defeated by 120 votes to 11.

The grass roots had spoken.

The first efforts to remove the ban started in 1924. For three years in-a-row, the Ban was voted on at Congress and prevailed every time – a new nation was in no mood to embrace anything outside of gaelic origin, even if the roots predated this new-fangled 'gaelic football'. Hurling is a genuinely ancient game – PJ Devlin was not far wrong when he said that 'the Gaels of Ireland were hurling when the gods of Greece were young'.

A motion reached Congress in 1962 to have the Ban removed but was rejected by 140 votes to 80; it had already been rejected in Kerry by a unanimous vote. That wasn't really a surprise.

John Joe Sheehy was a huge proponent of the Ban – it is well worth noting that despite their political opposition, the two men had great personal respect for each other. A motion against the Ban was defeated again in 1965, 230 votes to 52. Incoming President Seamus Ó Riain was another conservative in regards to the Ban. In 1968 it was upheld again... 220 to 88.

By now, though, Tom Woulfe's campaign to end the Ban was gathering steam, and the Civil Service clubman in Dublin was helped by writers like Eamon Mongey, Paddy Downey and Seán Óg Ó Ceallacháin. In 1970, a Mayo motion to hold a referendum among all clubs about the Ban (Rule 27) was passed.

On Easter Sunday, 1971, the Ban was finally removed from the GAA's rules.

The irony of it all was that soccer was still very popular in Ireland. The rapidly deteriorating political situation in Northern Ireland may have been making most of the headlines, but plenty of Irish people had as many friends and relatives in places like London and Liverpool than in their home parish because of emigration.

Furthermore, England's World Cup win in 1966 had been followed in 1970 by the most dazzlingly skilful, exuberant Brazilian team of all time, spearheaded by a young Pelé. People loved it, especially because they could watch it on their television screens.

Having good quality English games on the television saw a huge increase in the popularity of the likes of Liverpool, Everton, Manchester United, Arsenal and Leeds. Shamrock Rovers, Bohemians, Cork... they all looked passé in comparison, especially with the substandard facilities.

Even so, the Irish team had a hard core of support (and enough talent, albeit moulded in English fields) to have achieved far more success, but the lack of organisation at local or national level proved fatal.

Mick Meagan had been appointed Republic of Ireland manager in 1969, having the power to over-rule a selection committee of FAI appointees (most of them businessmen who certainly weren't watching many actual games of soccer) but in 1971 Ireland were already hitting rock bottom of the table in qualifying for the 1972 European Championships.

When the GAA first introduced Rule 27, soccer was a very real threat to the fledgling sport's existence.

By the time it was lifted? Not so much.

The Kerry team which claimed the All-Ireland title in 1970, and Donie has the great honour of lifting the Sam Maguire Cup on behalf of the people of Spa and Kerry.

« CHAPTER 11 »

IRELAND HOSTED THE Eurovision Song Contest in 1971, after Dana's victory the year before, and pulled out all the stops; it was RTÉ's first colour broadcast. Ireland needed something to cheer itself up, because a lot of the news was bad. Internment without trial was introduced in Northern Ireland amid severe rioting in Belfast – 1970 was the year of the Arms Crisis, when government ministers were charged with attempting to illegally import arms for nationalists in Northern Ireland to defend themselves against Loyalist mobs. They were tried, Charlie Haughey amongst them, and found not guilty.

The government survived a motion of no confidence.

Between collapsing trials and hinted allegations and frantic 'move on, nothing to see here', desperate attempts to preserve a modicum of dignity and, much more importantly, the fragile peace that still existed in the North, it was not our proudest moment.

A recently elected MP for North Antrim and firebrand unionist preacher named Rev Ian Paisley was not slow to take advantage as he established a new political party, the DUP.

An even bigger talking point for people was the introduction of decimalisation. It may have happened on Valentine's Day, but there was strong resistance to it at first, with people feeling that their money had been unfairly devalued.

FROM THE OUTSIDE, of course, football would always get the headlines, but football was only a very small part of Donie's life at the time. He got a teaching position in Tralee, in September of 1971. He and Áine welcomed their first child, Colm.

'There was less travel, for starters, and while I never minded coming home for games from Dublin, it is different when you are married, with family responsibilities.

'I enjoyed being back with the club here more of the time than ever before too.

'*Every year is a bonus…* that was my thinking at the time, and Johnny (Culloty) was training Kerry, and I had confidence and great trust in him, of course.

'We rented a house in Ardfert for eight or nine months, to begin with… our next door neighbours were Bill and Sheila McCarthy, who played minor football and hurling for Cork, and also hurled with Kerry for years. We have remained family friends ever since.

'There were pluses and minuses to coming back to Kerry after 10 years, but I was glad I did it. I'd been away… but, I suppose, you never really *leave*!

'My mother and father were in reasonably good health then too, and it was nice to be back close to them again.

'Also, there were a lot of teaching jobs back then, in the early 70s… it was easy to get one.'

The All-Ireland champions made a fantastic start to the National League. They beat Dublin by 0-16 to 2-4, Longford by 4-12 to 2-7, and Roscommon by 4-11 to 2-10. To be fair, Kerry were taking the league more seriously than other counties. Except Cork.

Cork were stung by the previous year's defeat in the Munster final, especially at how tamely they had gone down. Kerry had almost a full-strength team out in Cork on November 29 – O'Connell the only major absentee – and it made no difference. Cork won by 4-7 to 1-5.

Both counties knew it for a marker laid down.

Kerry followed that up with a draw in February, 2-5 apiece, against their other bogey team of the era, that great Offaly side. Wins over Galway and Kildare put them into a play-off against Dublin.

Dublin had lost the 1971 league semi-final to Mayo, but Dublin was not the force they had been. They did have good players. David Hickey had scored 2-1 in their first game in the 1970 Leinster Championship and Jimmy Keaveney had kicked 0-3. Tony Hanahoe had kicked a point. Dublin had put up a very creditable 3-8 total against Longford.

But it was also their last game in the Leinster Championship, because Longford had scored 2-14. Moreover, that was not an unexpected result.

Dublin were not considered a serious threat by anyone in the early-70s, a view shared by most Dubliners. Offaly and Meath were the big dogs in Leinster, with the likes of Longford and Kildare on their heels.

Keaveney had won a Leinster final in 1965 in his first year with the Dublin seniors. He hadn't even reached one since. In fact, in 1973 he would retire, frustrated not just by the lack of success but the lack of a desire to change it in Dublin.

That would have been that, but for a neighbour's child innocently recommending a full-forward to new Dublin manager Kevin Heffernan…

DERRY IN THE league semi-final was a different proposition.

It was a cracking game in Croke Park and a brilliant one despite the lashing rain. Seán O'Connell cemented his reputation as one of the best footballers in Ireland. But so did the Kerry captain – Donie was brilliant from wing back.

He had to be, and so did every player around him. DJ Crowley plundered 1-1 from midfield (there was a bit of luck about his first-half goal). Kerry clung on to a one-point lead in a game that pulsed from start to finish, 1-10 to 1-9.

Mayo were the reigning champions and in no mood to surrender their title easily. After all, they had played in 10 finals between 1934 and '70, and never lost. They opened in a whirlwind; genuinely awesome.

But so were the Kerry defence. Donie, Paud O'Donoghue and Seamus Mac Gearailt kept winning every ball that came their way. Des Griffith did manage to get through, but the crossbar saved Kerry. Willie McGee was quick onto the rebound – but Donie was amazingly faster and made a brilliant interception. It was electrifying.

Mayo tormented Kerry out the field but were spectacularly rebuffed every time they tried to turn possession into football currency on the scoreboard. All they had to show for it were frees by Joe Corcoran, and not many of them.

With them putting pressure on Mayo players in possession, Kerry began to get a grip on the game. Points from Donie, Brendan Lynch, and Mick O'Dwyer gave Kerry a 0-7 to 0-5 lead at half-time. Lynch, O'Dwyer and Mick Gleeson extended it after the break. In the end, Kerry were winners by 0-11 to 0-8.

Tom Morrison, in his book *For the Record* that chronicles the National Leagues in both hurling and football, would later observe that *Nobody epitomised Kerry's determination and self-belief more than the Spa captain whose tremendous display inspired his colleagues.*

That set Kerry up nicely for the championship.

Tipperary were game as always, but still well behind the top two in Munster. Dual player Michael 'Babs' Keating got a good goal for them (Babs, like teammate Jack Ryan from Moneygall, was so good a hurler that people tend to forget that he was also a genuinely brilliant footballer) and Paudie Blythe landed four points, but Mick O'Dwyer kicked 1-6 and Brendan Lynch had 0-4. Realistically, it was a job done, nothing more. Kerry eyes were focused on Cork.

Cork had dropped Denis Coughlan.

Most Cork supporters and many of the players were shocked at the decision, especially after Coughlan, one of the greatest dual players of all-time (Glen Rovers colleague Christy Ring was a big admirer) had fully committed to the footballers for 1971.

Kerry just shrugged and got down to work. By half-time they were leading by 0-11 to 0-7, with only Kevin Jer O'Sullivan and Humphrey Kelleher giving real resistance.

Then Cork brought Coughlan on after the break and he just could not be stopped.

He finished with 0-10.

Ray Cummins had 0-6.

Cork had a total of 0-25.

Kerry could only manage a miserable five points after half-time. Cork went on to lose to Offaly, who beat a fading and slightly wasteful Galway in the All-Ireland final.

DONIE'S COUNTY YEAR wasn't quite over. The Cúchulainn Awards had been instigated in 1963 and Donie had been awarded one in 1965. But this year the whole set-up was formalised into the All Stars scheme, with a formal banquet for the presentations (Jack Lynch handed over the silverware) and an overseas trip for the chosen teams. The GAA's hand had been forced into instigating the scheme in a way.

In January, the United Irish Societies of San Francisco had invited a specific team of 'All Stars' (an informal title) to play Kerry in March. They wanted to promote gaelic games; no better way to do it than have the biggest names in the game (they specified the players they wanted very carefully to attract maximum promotion, most especially three-time All-Ireland winner Seán O'Neill of Down) and they paid all expenses.

The team to play Kerry was: Billy Morgan (Cork); John Carey (Mayo), Jack Quinn (Meath), Andy McCabe (Cavan); Brian McEniff, John Morley (Mayo), Pat Reynolds (Meath); Bernie O'Neill (Cork), Ray Carolan (Cavan); Liam Sammon (Galway), Colm McAlarney (Down), Jimmy Duggan (Galway); Tony Brennan (Meath), Seán O'Neill (Down), and Declan O'Carroll (Donegal).

Players stayed with local families and San Francisco's tourism budget paid for the promotion. The All Stars won the first game well, but Kerry trained hard and won the second game the following Sunday.

It was a huge success and was sure to repeated.

In the circumstances, the GAA knew that they had to either refute the idea of 'All Stars' – which was sure to be resented by both players and their hosts – or adopt the scheme under their own control.

The whole thing was sponsored by PJ Carroll's, the cigarette company. Tobacco sponsorship was crucial to sport, not just in Ireland, but everywhere in the 70s. That was just reality. To be recognised among your peers is a huge thing. Journalist Mick Dunne organised it at the end of the year.

For the record, that official All Star team of 1971 was: PJ Smyth (Galway); Johnny Carey (Mayo), Jack Cosgrove (Galway), Donie O'Sullivan (Kerry); Eugene Mulligan (Offaly), Nicholas Clavin (Offaly), Pat Reynolds (Meath); Liam Sammon (Galway), Willie Bryan (Offaly); Tony McTague (Offaly), Ray Cummins (Cork), Mickey Kearins (Sligo); Andy McCallin (Antrim), Seán O'Neill (Down), Séamus Leydon (Galway).

But by the time those awards were presented, Donie did have an All-Ireland medal in his pocket.

Not with Kerry, but with East Kerry.

EAST KERRY HAD beaten Waterville in the 1970 county final for three Bishop Moynihan trophies on the trot.

The GAA had started a provincial club competition in 1964 and it had been a big success, with Shannon Rangers winning the first title. You must remember that all through Donie's era, the idea of a county team holding back players from club games was rare. It did happen, but it always tended to raise an outcry.

After all, the first All-Irelands had been played by the county championship-winning teams, not county selections. The club was the bedrock and the corner-stone of the association – and, to be blunt and honest about the modern approach, back then it wasn't just lip service.

When a motion to introduce an All-Ireland Club Championship came before Congress in 1969 (the Ulster and Connacht champions had played an unofficial 'final' since 1968), there was some opposition, but it got the two-thirds majority it needed.

The Munster final against Muskerry was a very tight affair, with East Kerry just about scraping through by 0-10 to 0-9. Gracefield from Offaly were the All-Ireland semi-final opponents, but East Kerry were able to maintain control in that one to set up the first-ever All-Ireland club final against Bryansford of Down.

Bryansford was a small club with a tight panel. In 1969 they had been plying their trade in Division Three of Down football. They had a great manager in Seán 'The Master' Smith though, and great footballers like Eugene Grant, Oliver Burns, the Neeson and Cunningham brothers, Seán O'Hare and John Joe Boden in goal. They also played an exciting brand of fluid attacking football that had seen off St John's of Belfast and Armagh's Crossmaglen in the Ulster semi-final.

Kerry had played Down three times in Croke Park in championship football by then (1960, '61 and '68), and never beaten them.

The game was refereed by Jimmy Hatton of Wicklow, who had refereed both the football and hurling All-Ireland finals in 1966. This was one of the easier days to be a referee.

Bryansford were slow to settle to the vastness of Croke Park. East Kerry, on the other hand, were out of the traps like lightning. They surged into a 10-point lead after 10 minutes. Bryansford did settle, but realistically it was all over. Mick Gleeson and Donal Kavanagh had two goals each and Denis Coffey a green flag of his own.

It was the first All-Ireland club title.

It would also be the last for a divisional team, as they were deemed ineligible by Congress a year later. Colleges were and still are allowed – Jim Gleeson, Denis Coffey, Donal Kavanagh and Niall Brosnan would fall just short of repeating the feat the following year when UCC were beaten by Bellaghy of Derry.

East Kerry would not be in contention to reclaim their title, however. On September 12, 1971, they lost out to Shannon Rangers in an absolute cracker of a county quarter-final by 3-9 to 2-10.

It was a brilliant game of football. It was also Donie's first defeat in the county championship in four years.

IF TENSIONS IN Northern Ireland were very high in 1971, the battle-lines were drawn for real in early '72, when the Parachute Regiment of the British Army opened fire on a peaceful march against internment without trial. Fourteen innocent people died. It wasn't just Ireland reeling from the atrocity; the famous photo of Fr Edward Daly waving a bloody handkerchief at an armed British soldier as he tried to tend to a dying man cradled in his lap went all around the world.

In the GAA world, things got a little bit easier, or maybe a little bit more challenging, with the introduction of the O'Neill's football. It was lighter and more aerodynamic than the old 'pigskin' football (it wasn't pigskin, it was always cowhide). The GAA established a committee chaired by former president Padraig McNamee to internally review the GAA. In December, the McNamee Report was published.

It proposed major improvement works to Croke Park, which had been virtually untouched since 1959 at a time when sports stadia all across Europe were being modernised – the advent of TV sponsorship was a big factor. The GAA were quick to approve of sponsorship in Croke Park.

As to whether that was a very slight incline or the start of a very slippery slope for an amateur organisation... well, history will judge. Ironically, the McNamee Report was strongly opposed to All-Ireland finals being televised because of a perceived impact on attendances.

Proposals for an open draw in inter-county hurling, while retaining the two viable provincial championships (Munster and Leinster) and, radically, an open draw in football without the provincial championships, were very hurriedly cast aside.

The GAA was not that ready to embrace change!

None of those were the big sports stories of the year.

In July, Muhammad Ali came to Croke Park to fight Al 'Blue' Lewis. It was an absolute sensation, comparable only to the arrival of JFK in 1963 (coincidentally, the same year that Ali had changed his name from Cassius Clay).

Ali was handsome, charismatic, and very different. In the TV Age, charisma was as important as talent, and Ali had plenty of both. He came, smiled, and joked with the Irish – and we adored him.

The fight, in which his long-time sparring partner and friend Blue Lewis clung on past a hard-fought fifth to go all the way to the eleventh round, was almost superfluous to the event.

KERRY PLAYED THREE Munster teams in the first three rounds of the National League and did not need to break sweat. Waterford and Tipperary were never expected to challenge hard in winter games, but a 2-12 to 1-5 victory over Cork was a little deceptive; Kerry had a very strong team out.

They got their first reverse against Offaly, their greatest rivals in the era. A week before Christmas, they lost to Dublin, of all teams. No big deal, really.

It wasn't even a blip on the radar back then.

Spring.

Back to business.

Kerry needed a win over Galway in Killarney to get back on the rails, and got it. They had Derry in the semi-final, and a *good* Derry team. They never quite made it to the top in that era, but they went very close – any team that did beat them had their work cut out to do it.

Kerry pulled clear in the finish to win by four points.

In the end, it was the same two teams from last year still standing, Kerry and Mayo. No wonder, then, that 32,000 people came to Croke Park to watch them. Kerry went four up before Mick O'Connell sent a beautiful ball into the forwards. The ball came back off the post but the elusive Mick Gleeson was a hawk at pouncing on such rabbit chances and JJ Costello had no chance on the rebound.

Mayo's greatest trait is that they, quite simply, never give up.

Tommy O'Malley was outstandingly defiant and showed his teammates the way. Willie McGee scored a great goal and by half-time they were back in it,

1-7 to 1-4. After 10 minutes of the second-half they were level and McGee had narrowly missed another goal chance.

It was Kerry's turn to right the ship with the game in the balance – two points from O'Connell put them on their way.

Mayo kept hammering at the door, but Kerry's seasoned defence just about had their measure.

An opportunist goal by Liam Higgins late on settled the issue.

TIPPERARY IN THE Munster Championship gave Kerry a decent game, but it was never in doubt. Cork, as always, was the big one.

Cork had a young, fit team primed for an 80-minute final.

Kerry led by two points at half-time but Donal Kavanagh and Mick Gleeson struck for goals early in the second-half and, although it was nip and tuck after that in play, Cork just couldn't get enough momentum to whittle down that lead.

Roscommon had been training in their newly opened Dr Hyde Park and they had good footballers. Mickey Freyne was as good as any footballer in the country and he would go on to win an All Star that year, Roscommon's first, and deserve it. Dermot Earley had played minor, under-21 (where he won an All-Ireland at midfield) and senior in 1966 and was an established Railway Cup star.

But success at inter-county level had always been denied to the county supporters. Life was to change for them and for Dermot Earley in 1972, when they beat Mayo to win their first Connacht title in a decade.

The county, naturally, was ecstatic, but they weren't quite ready to take the next step and while they gave Kerry an honest test, experience meant that it was never really in doubt.

There were young lads in Roscommon, though, who had gotten to watch a Roscommon man lift a Nestor Cup – small seeds like that can take hold. It would be later in the decade that those lads like 'Jigger' O'Connor and Tony McManus would take the lessons onto the field of play.

Offaly again.

Of course, it was going to be Offaly.

This time both sides knew each other and were ready.

Perhaps, as often happens, they knew each other too well. The weather was dull, and after a drawn game, John D. Hickey of the *Independent* described as 'colourless as the grey skies'. Offaly led late on but Kerry took the game to a replay.

It was a short-lived reprieve.

There was only one team in it on the second day, and it wasn't Kerry. They actually led by two points early in the second-half, but gave up a ridiculously soft goal, as a long ball by Paddy Fenning spun off the ground into the goal.

That was just a mishap, but the way it seemed to deflate Kerry while lifting the majestic Willie Bryan to new heights was telling. In the end, it was 1-19 to 0-13, Kerry's worst defeat in a final.

Kerry did reach the under-21 All-Ireland final, thanks to Paudie O'Mahony saving a late penalty from Derry's Martin O'Neill in the semi-final. There was no happy ending, though, for the likes of O'Mahony, Jimmy Deenihan, Mickey Ned O'Sullivan, Jackie Walsh, John Egan, or talented full forward Martin Ferris.

They were well beaten by Galway, 2-6 to 0-7.

IT'S HARD TO explain just how big the Railway Cup was from the 40s to the late 70s. It certainly wasn't as big as the All-Ireland itself, and would have played second fiddle to most, but not all, provincial finals.

But it dwarfed anything else in the public consciousness. All of the big players wanted to play in the Railway Cup. It wasn't just a means of representing your province, it was effectively an acknowledgement of your elite status.

It also meant that great players from weaker counties could play with and against their sporting peers on an equal footing. Mickey Kearns and Barnes Murphy of Sligo, and Brendan Barden and Seán Murray of Longford… they fully deserved every bit of limelight they got.

Christy Ring was, and still is, the most famous of them all.

Ring played Railway Cup for a whopping 23 years and won 18 Railway hurling medals with Munster. Des 'Snitchie' Ferguson of Dublin wasn't far behind. In 1962, he became the only player to win Railway hurling and football titles on the one day as Leinster completed a double.

Donie was an ever-present on Munster's Railway Cup teams from 1964 to '74. The only year season missed was 1966-67, when he was domiciled in the US, studying in St John's University. He had never won it, though.

Munster were as bad at the football as they were dominant in the hurling.

The last time that Munster had won the Railway Cup for football, Donie had been nine years old. Stars of that team had included Weeshie Murphy, Paddy Bawn Brosnan, Batt Garvey, Eamonn Young, and Jackie Lyne.

Munster had a good team in 1972. Of course, they did; everyone knew it. Billy Morgan had taken over Johnny Geraghty of Galway and Johnny Culloty of Kerry's mantle as the foremost custodian in the country.

Donie was a reigning All Star; compatriot Seamus Mac Gearailt was no novice either. On the square was one of the unheralded giants of the game from a county that never really had the numbers or public support in football, but had all the heart and courage of the bigger teams.

Big Jim Wall was part of the heart and soul of a Waterford team that had played in Division One in 1971. They drew with Kildare and Galway and went within a single point of Cork. In the half-back line you had the 1970 Footballer of the Year Tom Prendergast.

Kevin Jer O'Sullivan, who had many great years in the Cork jersey, had been a very surprising omission from the All Star team, having kicked two '50s' and given a football exhibition in the 1971 Munster final. His son Brendan Jer would follow him into a Cork jersey later.

Mick O'Connell was partnered by Frank Cogan in midfield. Donal Hunt and Eamonn O'Donoghue flanked Denis Coughlan in the half forward line, with Hunt wearing the captain's armband.

Babs Keating and Ray Cummins would later be more famous as hurlers, but they were brilliant footballers.

But everybody knew that a lot of good Munster teams had come home empty-handed since 1949, and there were no great indicators that it was about to change. No matter, the crowds flocked anyway.

The Railway Cup final, a chance to see the best players in the country in action?

What else would you be doing on the day that's in it?

Munster had a tough semi-final against Connacht in the Athletic Grounds on February 20, before prevailing on a 1-9 to 0-9 scoreline. That put them into the final on St Patrick's Day in Croke Park against Leinster, and that was a formidable team.

Willie Bryan of Offaly was captain. Offaly were always going to dominate that

Leinster team, just as Kerry would provide the main components for Munster. Martin Furlong, Mick Ryan, Eugene Mulligan, Niall Clavin, Kevin Kilmurray, Tony McTeague, Seán Cooney, John Smith on the bench... all great Offaly players. Bobby Millar of Laois partnered Bryan in the middle. Ken Rennicks and Mickey Fay of Meath were in the forwards. Tommy Carew and Pat Mangan of Kildare were there as well; Kildare had a great team at the time as well.

It was indicative of Dublin's place in the pecking order of Leinster GAA that they had no player on the starting 15, although Paddy Cullen and Frank Murray were on the bench.

It was always going to be close between those two teams.

In fact, they proved inseparable on the day, at 1-15 apiece. Munster's equalising point was spectacular. It was Frank Cogan who won the free, a full 55 metres out. As Donie says, 'Mick O'Connell didn't even place the ball. He just looked at it where it lay, stepped up, and sent it straight between the posts.

'It might sound strange, because that was a difficult kick for any other player, but every single onlooker simply knew beforehand that he was going to do that.

'That's a simple measure of how good he was.'

It took almost a month to arrange the replay back in Cork. There are similarities between an inconvenience and an opportunity at times. In this case, the wait for the extra game meant that the Munster team spent more time together than was usual for Railway Cup players and it helped to forge a close bond that remains to this day.

By the time of the replay, they were raring to go and over 30,000 supporters filled the Athletic Grounds. Munster claimed the title at the second attempt, and Donie was especially grateful to finally pick up a Railway Cup medal.

'We only won it once, so we were going to remember it,' he emphasises.

'We put a lot of effort into it every year, but we weren't good enough, and if you look at the records so many good teams lost finals by only a couple of points.

'That was our story playing for Munster too.

'But we probably had our best team that year, and we prepared that bit better with training sessions. When we drew with Leinster in the final, the lads became very anxious about winning it at the second attempt.

'That team resulted in a good number of friendships too... Denis Coughlan and Ray Cummins were on the team, and we have never lost touch since.

'I have no idea why the GAA let the Railway Cup go and finally disappear altogether. It was great for the so-called weaker counties, but all of the players loved getting together with different lads from different counties.

'It served players well over the years.'

Back home, East Kerry lost out to Laune Rangers in the county championship quarter-final. East Kerry were not and would not be the force they had been for many years to come, not least because a second divisional team named Eoghan Ruadh (after Eoghan Ruadh Ó Suilleabháin from Sliabh Luachra, one of the four Kerry poets) to cater for Rathmore, Gneeveguilla, Glenflesk and Kilcummin players.

DR JIM BROSNAN, arguably the greatest county chairman Kerry ever had, stepped down. His focus had never been on Kerry winning All-Irelands only, though he had been part of that happening in his days both as a player and as an administrator.

He had introduced coaching programmes and developed facilities to establish a broad base of players, not just supporters. Perhaps even more significantly, he appointed Fr Seamus Linnane, principal of St Brendan's College, to form a Bórd na nÓg for juveniles.

It was, and still is, a huge success.

Community Games also started that year in Tralee and were organised county-wide. Although not connected at all to the GAA, the two bodies were to form a natural symbiosis that were to have a profound effect for young people in Kerry for many years to come and are still going strong.

Timmy Joe O'Sullivan, Tadhg O'Sullivan, Archie Cronin, and Joe McAuliffe (future Kerry footballer Mike's father) established it in Spa and did their job well.

Donie says of the Moyvane native and Dingle icon who re-shaped Kerry GAA in a more all-inclusive image that, 'I believe there was nobody more important in the over-all picture of the GAA in this county for his vision, his commitment, his generosity, and his work rate; he was such an upright, humble and honourable man, direct to the point.

'We all experienced in that trip around the world in 1970 the type of leadership he showed and that generosity he expounded.

'Jim listened to people who played the game, he always had a vision and when he became chairman, he put that vision into practice… that of getting more and more players on the field.

'Getting the leagues going. He began it, followed it through and it went on from there.'

Kerry photographed in 1972, but their bid to win back Sam Maguire was stopped as Offaly retained their All-Ireland title after a replay.

« CHAPTER 12 »

THE VIETNAM WAR ended in 1973 when the US came to its senses, having lost as much because of public opposition back home, as the obduracy of the Viet Cong. American Secretary of State Henry Kissinger received the Nobel Prize for Peace – songwriter Tom Lehman famously said 'Political satire became obsolete when Henry Kissinger was awarded the Nobel peace prize'.

This was the year that Billie Jean King beat Bobby Riggs in a tennis match billed as 'The Battle of the Sexes'. It was very much about the billing; Riggs deliberately over-hyped and blustered at will – that would be a common trait in professional sports in the 70s.

Many sports promoters were trying to engage people's interest in the same way as Muhammed Ali had – but none of them were Ali. Over in Castleisland, Mick Fitzgerald was one of those who was watching that tennis match.

Ladies football was in its infancy, having started as participation in tournaments in Offaly in the late-60s and slowly spread. It had arrived in Cork and Waterford as organised formal championships in 1971 – Kerry cailíní weren't going to be kept away from the game. Fitzgerald and Scotsman Alex Rintoul set up a Kerry team that took on Cork in a challenge game as part of a North Cork Festival – 2,000 people showed up.

Cork GAA star Denny Long agreed to referee and was a big draw, and they were treated to a great spectacle. Cork's Bridie Brosnan was already well-known and proved that her reputation was fully deserved, but young Mary Geaney scored 2-6 in Kerry's 5-10 to 4-11 win.

It was the start of a great inter-county rivalry to match the men's game and one that continues to this day.

Back in the early-70s, Kerry people were not expecting any ladies team to be making headlines, though! That was very much the male preserve, and all eyes were, of course, on one particular team. The 1969 and '70 All-Ireland triumphs were ancient history.

That bread was already eaten, and Kerry supporters were hungry again.

KERRY SCRAPED PAST Roscommon in the National League by a single point and lost away to Longford in their first two games. But they beat Cork, and that calmed the supporters.

Wins against Offaly, Kildare, and, of course, perennial underdogs Dublin meant that a loss to Galway in an abysmal game didn't matter. They drew against Derry in the semi-final but Derry, for very obvious reasons amid the turmoil in Northern Ireland, couldn't field in the replay. That put Kerry into the league final against none other than Offaly.

This was the kind of team Kerry wanted to meet.

Tony McTeague would finish with 0-12 on the day. But Kerry's full back line of Donie, Paud O'Donoghue and young Jimmy Deenihan gave an absolute exhibition of top-class defending, both individually and as a synchronised unit. McTeague was the only Offaly forward to score.

The Faithful County were still a brilliant team, but not the force that they had been. Brendan Lynch scored a goal to put Kerry in front after 15 minutes and added another one before half-time. Kerry led by 2-4 to 0-8 but were lucky that Kevin Kilmurry's shot had skinned just wide off the Kerry post.

Offaly made some good switches in the second-half and managed to nudge back in front by a point, with Willie Bryan leading the way despite the best efforts of a young Kerry midfield of Donal Kavanagh and John O'Keeffe.

But while they could match Kerry almost everywhere on the field, there was one crucial area where they just couldn't make headway. Brendan Lynch was Man of the Match, no question about it, but it was Kerry's full back line that won the county's third National League title on the trot.

The Munster semi-final in Tralee against Tipperary was always going to be a formality, and so it proved. It was a comfortable outing for Donie and his colleagues, with Tipperary only able to muster 0-5 in total. To be honest, nobody was overly interested in the appetiser.

The entree was being served in the Athletic Grounds, and that was the game everybody wanted to see. Get past Cork, and there was an All-Ireland for the taking.

It actually started well for Kerry.

But Donie Donovan had trained Cork well and, just as importantly, he had devised the correct tactics for the day that was in it. Teams had always adopted game plans and match-ups that would suit their own strengths; Down in the early 60s being the most obvious example, but the 1973 Munster final was an exemplary demonstration of their effectiveness.

Cork out-foxed Kerry, and did it brilliantly.

Donie, like others, knew that Cork had a very good team in the making. 'One didn't have to be a seer to predict a big Cork breakthrough from the 1960s,' he explains. 'They had produced great minor and under-21 teams, and these players became the backbone of their senior team at the start of the 70s.

'Some of us, who were pushing on, we relieved to have won Munster in 1969 and '70.'

Kerry had always expected Ray Cummins to move into his usual role at full-forward and engage in a hard physical battle with Paud O'Donoghue – the pair were old foes, who were great friends off the pitch. That was how they lined out for the throw-in (counties were fined for late changes to the named programme back then).

Except that Ray didn't stay in full-forward, he went just off to the right on the half-forward line.

Cork's sprinting greyhounds left up front didn't even look at each other, didn't want to give the game away. Kerry's square was open space now. Cork's outfield players knew where to put the ball.

Dinny Long sent a long ball in. He wasn't passing it; he was aiming for the empty space. By the time the ball arrived, so did Declan Barron; he had started running before it had left Dinny's boot.

BANG!

Goal number one.

Jimmy Barrett pounced for goal number two.

A penalty, smoothly converted by Billy Field. Goal number three.

Kevin Jer O'Sullivan and Con Hartnett were quick onto every loose ball. A speculative Cork shot came back off the upright and a teenage Jimmy Barry Murphy deftly trapped it soccer-style and neatly stabbed it home.

Goal number four.

There was almost an inevitability about it when Jimmy Barrett rose highest in the square to fist home his second and number five for a rampant Cork.

A goal every six minutes.

By half-time it was 5-4 to 0-6.

Cork were in no hurry coming back out after the break. *Why would they be?* Kerry did improve in the second-half, with Jackie Walsh making a big difference when he went to midfield. John Egan and Dwyer picked off points, and Donal Kavanagh burst through for a goal. Billy Field and Jimmy Barrett replied, but Egan picked off another one.

The gap was down to five points.

Frank Cogan stalwart Denis Coughlan steadied Cork's ship and brought it over the line.

Cork 5-12 Kerry 1-15.

Some days taste of nectar. Some days taste of ashes. The strange thing is that Kerry hadn't actually played that badly. Kerry teams had played worse overall and won matches; 1-15 would win you a lot of games. But Cork, especially those ravenous forwards… they were something special.

Cork put another five goals past Tyrone in the All-Ireland semi-final and prepared for Galway in the final. They had last won the football All-Ireland back in 1945. Sadly, Weeshie Murphy, one of the stars of that victory and father to Dr Con, passed away shortly before the final. Jimmy Barry Murphy scored a goal early on against Galway and added another near the finish.

Billy Morgan lifted the Sam Maguire.

IF THAT DEFEAT to Cork meant that it was considered a bad year for Kerry, it was a great one for Spa, and Donie remembers it far better than the Munster final.

Flights were affordable for ordinary people for nigh on the first time ever, and Spa decided to travel as a club to the United States, where of course they, like pretty much everyone in Ireland, had very strong links.

That was a massive undertaking at the time… far, far bigger than it is nowadays. It was audacious, to say the least.

Preparations began in 1972. Paul O'Sullivan, Tadhg's son, was free for the summer and devoted a huge amount of time into arranging the details. Donie called many of his contacts in New York (of which he had, of course, many).

Remember, this is a time before email, let alone mobile phones.

While the likes of Donie and Mick Gleeson with Kerry, or Pat Casey with the Navy, would be seasoned travellers, most of the party probably hadn't left Ireland before.

Counihan's Travel in Killarney were able to offer return flights from Shannon to New York for £59 – and Spa chartered a Pan Am plane through the travel agency. This was before the Arab-Israeli Yom Kippur War in 1973 which drove oil prices worldwide through the roof.

There was no question of booking hotels – beds were arranged with various friends and families in New York. After all, this was at least as much about connecting with the people over there as anything else.

However, the enterprise and forethought in chartering the plane ensured that the club made a profit which was enough to fund the deposit for Spa's playing field.

Everyone recognised this as a massive opportunity, and seized it with both hands. Spa, however, would regroup and hit the States again with a smaller group a few years later.

This time, Spa were going to the west coast. It was again a fabulous trip – and again the generosity of their hosts knew no bounds.

Nor was it strictly confined to club members; the likes of Seán Óg Sheehy (Mitchels), Paudie Doolan (Kilcummin) and Denis Moynihan (Glenflesk) blended very easily into the company. Pat Kelleher, Donie O'Leary and John O'Leary (national award-winning PRO and still a key administrator for Kerry), Tim Regan, Pat Casey, Bernie O'Riordan, Neilie O'Doherty, Donie McSweeney, Jackie Foley, Seán Cronin of The Island, John O'Sullivan… you couldn't go wrong in that company.

They visited Universal Studios, Disneyland, the Golden Gate Bridge, Alcatraz… they saw all the sights and loved it. It was a special group – Donie especially recalls genial Dave Herlihy as the life and soul of the party.

They played some challenge games while there, of course.

They started with a Los Angeles selection in Orange County, a great chance for the Irish community in the whole area to come together... and they did.

A week later they played their hosts Shannon Rangers in the Balboa Stadium, and then both Spa and Rangers headed to Reno in Nevada to play another game in the Minogue Stadium.

It was the first-ever game of gaelic football played in the State of Nevada.

The local band played *When Irish Eyes Are Smiling* in the assumption that it was the Irish national anthem. Arrah, with the good humour that was prevailing, no one was too bothered – both teams sang along with cheerful gusto.

While there, Donie and a few more took a side tour to San Diego. Fr Jerry Murphy from Barradubh, whom Donie had known all his life, was stationed there. His curate was none other than Offaly's Fr Nicky Clavin, an old sparring partner of Donie's on the field of play and a good friend off it.

He was one of the great dual players in football and hurling, and a great handballer as well.

Another man that Donie met up with was Jim Foley from Keel, whom Donie had played with often in New York. Jim was one of the great unsung midfielders and a key player in New York's National League success in the 60s.

Donie liked San Diego – and the Irish community in San Diego easily absorbed him as one of their own. It was to have a greater significance in Donie's life that he might have expected.

'The first trip was the big one,' Donie remarks.

'The field was being purchased at the time, but they made some money. It was a charter flight... 45 pounds return, and there was profit in that because once you had so many passengers committed, you actually had the whole plane paid for.

'I was only with them on this trip for a weekend, Mick Gleeson likewise... I made up for that the second time we went to the America.

'We were back in school... but the others had three or four weeks out there and they had the time of their lives. And they made contact with so many people who had left Kerry in the 40s and 50s, old friends in Boston and New York especially.

'A club going on a trip like that, and reuniting with their own people out there, was a very special thing.

'The second trip in 1978... that was very different. We had fewer travellers in our party and, because of that, it was more ambitious is so many ways.

'In Nevada, we were the first GAA team to visit the state and play a game with the locals. We really pushed the boat out on that trip but our thinking was that, all the time people were hearing of rugby clubs going on long trips abroad...why not a small rural GAA club?

'Why not, indeed!

'It was a marvellous experience for us all, and the memories from those few weeks never faded. We played a good few games, including one in New York on our way home, but the game in Nevada was the special one.'

AT THE START of 1974, no one was betting against Cork to retain their All-Ireland; they were much more likely to add Liam McCarthy than to relinquish Sam Maguire.

Kerry had been great, but the years were taking their toll on some.

Offaly were not the force they had been. Kildare had a decent team, but not much more than that, and there were no other counties sticking out above the parapet.

Ulster was in turmoil – the political strife up there was being euphemistically called 'the Troubles' in much the same way that the greatest world war in human history had been referred to as 'the Emergency'.

Gaelic football had to strive harder against adversity there than anywhere else; they wouldn't be picking up any All-Irelands soon.

Dublin?

Sport in Dublin seemed to be in decline.

The crowds who had gone to League of Ireland soccer games were staying at home watching *Match of the Day* instead and looking to England for their heroes. Any lad who was good at soccer was taking the boat; that was Ireland's only development pathway.

The national team still had a hard core of city support, but a lack of success or decent administration wasn't going to attract any converts.

Rugby was actually of a high quality at the time. Big Moss Keane, who had played a little for Kerry and won a Sigerson with several of the players, was one of the big names in rugby. But rugby had a limited core of support from its base of fee-paying schools and colleges. It was a working-class game in Limerick, but the vast bulk of Dubliners were indifferent.

Lads weren't exactly desperate to play for Dublin. Gay O'Driscoll would later say, bluntly, that 'You didn't tell people that you played for Dublin'.

Jimmy Gray knew there was a problem, and privately he knew that the organisation of the county team was at the centre of it. Players had become accustomed to doing what they wanted, not what was needed.

Training sessions were about coaxing, not demanding. Gray decided to take action.

And Gray quite obviously had a man in mind to change things.

One Kevin Heffernan.

Heffernan was the new Dublin manager, with his friends Donal Colfer and Lorcan Redmond from the old management alongside him.

NOBODY IN KERRY was sweating over Dublin. They had enough to be worrying about with Cork.

Kerry knew at the start of the league that they had work to do. They won their first three league games no problem. All seemed right with the world. But Cork stole a march on them in Killarney to win by 1-6 to 0-8. A marker, but a good response, though; hammering none other than Offaly. Kerry beat Tipperary well, and drew with Galway. It was a good league for Kerry, one that engendered confidence in young legs.

They met Roscommon in the final.

Kerry led by 0-4 to 0-2 in the rain at half-time, and it could have been more if Paudie White hadn't made a superb save to deny Mikey Sheehy. With Mickey Freyne and John O'Gara on top at midfield, Roscommon went 0-8 to 0-4 clear at the three-quarter mark. The weather was making this difficult, and the underdog westerners were relishing the struggle. Kerry narrowed the gap, but it opened again and Roscommon were three points clear as the game entered injury time.

Mickey Ned O'Sullivan then laid the ball off to John Egan, who flicked home. A shell-shocked Roscommon had their celebrations very abruptly curtailed.

Roscommon matched Kerry toe-to-toe in the replay, but relied heavily on the brilliance of Dermot Earley to do so. Earley was deadly from frees and had to be; Paudie Lynch couldn't quite hold him in open play but went closer than most players ever did on the army man. Tom Heneghan had a goal disallowed for a push on Mahony, but they were reliant on frees for the most part. Heneghan and

Paud O'Donoghue had a tremendous duel, but Donie and young Paidí Ó Sé won virtually everything that came their way.

A quick scoring blitz saw Kerry kick five points in seven minutes to lead by 0-9 to 0-4 at the break. Roscommon kept coming, but again the Kerry defence, in which Donie was a linchpin, was the rock that their hopes perished on.

Kerry won by 0-14 to 0-8.

Kerry supporters basically just shrugged. That was four league titles in-a-row and six out of the previous seven, where there had previously been a drought. But, in truth, Kerry didn't want league titles; they wanted Sam Maguire coming back across the border, and nothing less was going to satisfy.

A FULL-FORWARD LINE of John Egan, Seamus Mac Gearailt and Mikey Sheehy scored 6-6 between them against a hapless Waterford. Nobody really cared too much on either side; this was a game to get out of the way. This year was all about Cork.

July 4 is Independence Day in America. But in 1974, in a Fitzgerald Stadium, such matters were only trivialities. This was where the action was happening. And it was not pretty.

It was a wet day, it was poor enough football all round, and there was no doubt whatsoever about who was the better team. Kerry led by two points at half-time but the second-half was disastrous.

Dave McCarthy slammed in a goal 10 minutes into the second-half. Cork had the self-belief and desire that Kerry lacked. O'Connell came off the bench, but Kerry were in trouble.

Mickey Ned got a second-half score with a minute left.

Contrary to popular myth nowadays, this was not an old Kerry team. In fact, the exact opposite. Johnny Culloty was a good judge of football always and only five veterans started the Munster final.

Three of them were in the full back line – Donie, Paud O'Donoghue and Derry Crowley. Paud's brother Eamonn was on the wing and Seamus Mac Gearailt, whose first match for Kerry back in 1963 had actually been as a goalkeeper, was a gamekeeper turned poacher at full-forward.

IN LEINSTER, DUBLIN had beaten Wexford and Louth. That was decent going, pike in a freshwater pool. But they were going swimming with a shark next; most Dublin people could have named more Offaly players than Dublin ones.

They led Offaly by a point at half-time. It was level pegging late on. Dublin were used to going out at the quarter-final stage in Leinster, and now they were in bonus territory.

In the last minute, Leslie Deegan launched one last monster effort that split the posts. Dublin had beaten Offaly!

A small few Dubs made a killing in the bookies, but very few – prophets are rarely recognised in their own land. Before that game Dublin had the inert mass and momentum of a tectonic plate. Afterwards, it was a blue avalanche that just wasn't going to slow down.

Kildare fancied their chances against the Dubs but were beaten by six points. Young Brian Mullins got the goal.

Hill 16 loved the skill of Mullins as much as the hard core. Meath in the final? Just like back in 1955. It was always going to be Meath. It had to be *Meath*. Over 37,000 people came to Croke Park, and most of them were Dubs.

The players left the Hill cheering after a five-point win. Cork, in the All-Ireland semi-final, were hot favourites against Dublin; they hadn't seen that rising tide and they were swamped by it.

Kerry far from Croke Park... touring the United States in the 1970s.

« CHAPTER 13 »

DONIE O'SULLIVAN KNEW that 1975 was his last hurrah.

A new era was beginning for Kerry football, not that many might have ever guessed at the beginning of '75 that it would include eight All-Ireland titles in the next 12 years.

Mick O'Dwyer was about to unveil a new team.

Those young footballers who had found the first half of the 70s troublesome as Kerry footballers would be on that team. Other young footballers would be found.

For Donie, who was asked to remain in the dressing-room, and guide and influence those around him, it was time to start counting down the months and weeks... and leave the room for god.

Donie felt okay with the finish line in sight.

He knew that he was slowing up for the top level. Just like in 1963 when he left Maynooth, Donie has always had the ability to move forward instead of looking back.

'At that age, the body lets you know what it thinks of things... and there's no lying to yourself. I had found that out in 1974, even at club level. I found it difficult and it dawned on me, like it dawns on everyone eventually, if they stay out there long enough, that I was just slowing up.

'There's no way out of it.

'I hadn't actually played for the county for a good while, but when they asked me to part of it in 1975, I agreed. I remember saying that I would not be up to it, but that I was more than happy to help out.

'It was a different involvement that year for me, and watching the team it was obvious that they didn't have that supreme confidence early on but... they got better and better.'

He played senior for Kerry 107 times, a number of appearances sitting behind only Mick O'Connell (129). More than medals, he brought the friendships with him, and they hold true to this day.

And not just Kerry friendships, either.

He could easily list a hundred famous names off the top of his head that he communicates with regularly... but he won't. First of all, he won't do that. And secondly, he wouldn't be sure or ever care in the slightest about the criteria for 'famous'.

He knows innately the criteria for friendship. They all do. Deep down at the root and soul of us all, it's what defines us as human.

'It was Murt Kelly who enticed me to stay, and help out through 1975, him an no one else. He was wonderfully shrewd and extremely intelligent, and I trusted him.

'I was happy to agree to his request, even if I did not get any games in the summer of 1975. That's not what it was about for me at the time. I didn't really want games. I always paid attention to Murt's counsel and expert advice. I think he was born with enlightenment.

'By the middle of 1974, I was well aware that I had *looked my last on youth.*'

Donie quotes from Wordsworth's *Tintern Abbey.*

That time is past

And all its aching joys are now no more...

'At a certain age,' he continues, ' the body lets one know the state of affairs, and there is no benefit in being in denial.

'I was aware that I was slowing down, not only in energy but also in reaction. It was becoming evident, even at club level.'

HOWEVER, THERE WAS still Spa, for a little time longer.

Donie's footballing year wasn't finished yet. Spa reached the O'Donoghue

Cup final, having beaten Rathmore and Dr Crokes by comfortable margins. Unfortunately, November 2 was a wet, windy day, and the ground was soft. In the circumstances, both Spa and Gneeveguilla acquitted themselves well, but the final could never really be described as a thriller.

Spa led by 0-5 to 0-3 at half-time. Denis Murphy blasted a great goal after half-time to put Gneeveguilla a point up, but Connie Doolan and Mick Gleeson reversed that, and Spa went on to win by 0-8 to 1-3.

They reached another O'Donoghue Cup final in 1976 (and won the intermediate title, beating Waterville in the final). This game was a thriller, but this time the result didn't go their way, with Killarney Legion winning by 2-10 to 2-6. Mick Gleeson and Tim O'Regan goaled at the start and end of the second-half. Donie's performance at corner-back proved that he was still one of the best footballers around.

Spa won it back in 1977.

THERE ARE ASPECTS of the modern game that Donie disapproves of strongly.

There is certainly an element of inclement professionalism in all but name. Very few players of his era made any profit as such from the game. It wasn't a business. Profit and loss were not the driving concerns they are today.

Sponsorship wasn't a factor.

The GAA made money in order to spend money on GAA activities. Gaelic games weren't a profit-making exercise – it was all about the promotion of a gaelic cultural identity.

Yes, you needed to make money on the biggest games, especially at inter-county level – but it was about developing facilities for clubs and communities. That was always the bottom line – is that really the case now? Donie certainly isn't the only one whose answer would be 'no'.

'I got plenty out of the game. I was wined and dined all over the world and not once was I asked to put my hand in my pocket. It was an incredibly enriching experience,' states Donie, matter-of-factly.

'Looking back, I would consider myself very fortunate.'

'Catch and kick' had been the emphasis in Kerry in Donie's playing days and long before them. To him – and many more of his generation – the game was played in such a way that skill dominated. Hand-passing to retain possession or blanket defences are anathema to him.

That doesn't mean that he isn't progressive, far from it. He worked all through his career at improving his playing, and that included understanding and adapting to new tactics and methods. Donie had always been interested in tactical awareness and understanding of the game from a young age, and turned his hand to coaching.

The rigid obedience to instructions of the modern era has never overly impressed him – in his playing days, Dr Eamonn had an emphasis on positioning, but players were expected to make decisions and adapt to circumstances on the field. Team managers tend to get the bulk of the praise for a victory and all of the blame for a defeat. In fact, once players cross the white line there is very little enough that a manager can do to influence a game – most of the work needs to have been done by then, especially in the inculcation of skill and understanding.

Ultimately, it's the best players on either team who will exert the most influence. That is a truism of all sports, and the best managers enable that while incorporating it into an overall structure. A coach's job is to prepare the players both physically and mentally to produce their best. Donie had always done that, either formally or informally, with the teams he had played on.

Donie loved thinking about the game and, as a teacher, was well able to communicate that to players. He trained Tralee RTC, and helped out a number of teams. He was the coach of the Kerry Vocational Schools team in their most successful era, including a young Jack O'Connor and Tommy Doyle, a student of Donie's in Tralee Community College.

His knowledge of the game was recognised at Munster level, too. The first coaching course in Munster was run by his old sparring partner and great friend, Eamonn Young. Johnny Culloty, Donie and Weeshie Fogarty used to travel up to Clare every Saturday, giving football lessons to the young fellas.

Ed O'Neill, teacher and sports co-ordinator at St Brendan's College, but back then a student in the RTC (now amalgamated with Cork RTC to form Munster IT), remembers Donie's coaching. 'We wouldn't have been great at all, to be honest about it. The RTC had very few sports grants. The Sigerson was confined to the National Universities (UCC, UCD UCG, and Trinity) in those days. But that never bothered Donie. He had fierce drive in him and he knew how to instil that. We respected him at the start of his first coaching session – we respected him even more afterwards.'

He was involved in the Kerry Techs from early on, and not just concentrating on coaching in his own school. He was also PRO of the Kerry Techs for a number of years and trained several of them to All-Irelands. In 1978 alone he worked with players like Jack O'Connor of Cahirsiveen, John Chute of Listowel, Ambrose O'Donovan, Donal Kelliher, and Donal Murphy of Rathmore, Joe Murphy of Castleisland, and James Sheehan and Peter Lyons of Killorglin – all of whom have gone on to coach teams successfully in their own right.

It was Liam Sayers who brought him on board – sure, how could you refuse Liam, who was the absolute heart and soul of the game.

THE 50s AND 60s were a golden era for newspaper sales. With increasing education standards and more business prospects, Irish people were paying more attention to national and international matters.

The biggest national papers were the *Irish Independent* and *The Irish Press*. Sports has always been a staple of newspapers, and most sporting bodies have quickly realised that co-operation with the media is an essential for popularising a sport.

The Irish Times was widely considered to be a pro-imperialist and Protestant paper – it wasn't quite fair, but it wasn't exactly wrong, either. The *Times* has tended to be conservative and pro-establishment. It had been the last national newspaper to acknowledge gaelic games as equal to the likes of rugby and cricket.

That attitude had changed by the 60s.

Peter Byrne, the *Times*' main sportswriter, who sadly passed away in August 2022, covered a myriad of disciplines including athletics, rugby, soccer and, of course, gaelic games and did it with a gently observant pen.

◄ ◄ ◆ ▷ ►

PETER BYRNE

We rarely spoke to players. It just wasn't done or expected. The likes of O'Connell was almost a mystical or mythological creature, rowing across from Valentia Island to play football as part of a way of life. We weren't going to be proving or deconstructing that myth. It wasn't all myth, either, O'Connell could put the ball on a sixpence from 50, 60, even 80 yards away. The likes of Mick Dunne, Paddy Purcell, John D., myself...

you'd almost be afraid to ask any questions of O'Connell, and of course, he is a quiet, shy man by nature. There was very little interaction between media and players It was only in later years that I got to know him and find out that, not only is he one of nature's gentlemen, but he also has a brilliant dry wit. Mind you, Tom Long was a footballer whose brilliance was under-estimated because of O'Connell; he was also one of the best footballers I ever saw in my life. O'Connell was unquestionably the Crown Prince of Football, but Tom Long was very, very nearly as good.

The funny thing is that Kerry football wasn't going great in those days – they hadn't actually won the All Ireland since 1962 – but they were still some of the most famous people in this country. Kerry had an aura about them. Donie was one of the players that epitomised that.

Donie never looked out of place on the Kerry team. He slotted in straightaway as if he had been there for years and he was an ever-present.

Like most footballers and hurlers back then, he never imposed himself consciously on people, but he was one of the best-known footballers in the country. His kicking ability was legendary, his only rival in that department was Mick Moylan from Dublin. In 1962 O'Connell was left three-quarters, O'Dwyer was on the forty, Donie O'Sullivan was midfield. That was how highly he was rated.

He played right and left full-back, left wing back, and midfield. Four All Ireland medals and two All Stars. He had the basic skills right from the start, but he never stopped developing as a footballer. You must remember that television was in its infancy and still a rare enough phenomenon.

What the national papers would cover in the early years was the All-Ireland semi-final and final, and it was limited enough coverage at that. People like Donie were able to impose themselves on the national psyche without pictures. In a curious way, they almost defined a certain sense of Irishness. Part of it was their attitude to football. Unlike ninety-eight percent of people who enjoyed success as a footballer and lived on that glory for the rest of their lives, Donie always saw his playing days as just one segment of his life. He never relied on his reputation as a footballer to achieve anything else.

He didn't care all that much about his All-Ireland medals; it was the friendships along the way that counted. You'd rarely find that attitude among recently retired sports people; most of them need to take some time to come to terms with it.

Donie is actually a very friendly man, and he liked talking to journalists. He has great respect for the written word. I don't believe he was meant for Maynooth, but it equipped him with a great classical education. He can quote Latin and Greek, and studied history and philosophy before going on to study sociology and psychology. Naturally the written word has an affinity for him and he was always willing to discuss the actual art of story-telling with us.

I mentioned to him one day that I'd heard that there are 155 different writing styles – between the pair of us, we still haven't come across them all yet!

He also has a great kindness to him.

When Pat Griffin was sick, Donie would regularly visit him. David Hickey from Dublin… they are great friends. Mattie McDonagh of Galway. He defined the Christian ethos in this country more than anyone. Not just a great player, which he most certainly was, he's an outstanding human being, and that's far more important.

When they talk of expanding the role of the laity in the Catholic Church, it would be hard to find a better example than Donie. He is identified with all the best things about the laity. It was a decision made in Heaven, I believe, to have him leave his studies for the priesthood.

Donie is apt to recall a memorable evening in California in 1972 as the start point of a long and valued relationship which would subsequently enrich his life. David Guiney and Paddy Downey, two the most respected sportswriters of their time, were in San Francisco to cover a Kerry match there and Donie was intrigued and entertained in equal measure as the conversation developed over the next three or four hours.

In an era when footballers and sports people generally tended to encounter journalists only on match days, it was an eye-opening if not ear-splitting experience for our man as the two Cork natives traded elements of the stories which had gone unreported at the time.

Downey, with an accent which was only rarely shared by people from his home village of Schull, possessed the vocabulary to bring new life to anecdotal tales which had been floating around since the earliest years of the GAA but which now sounded more vital and realistic than ever.

David Guiney's house contained the raw ingredients for the 'sessions' which, depending on the intake of liquid in those heady, pre-1980 days, could last well into the early hours and cover almost any topic along the way. David wasn't really a GAA person – more a member of that hardy breed of track and field people.

Donie O'Sullivan was just one of an established group of callers to the house with 'Duhallow' on its name-plate.

◄◄◆►►

THE GUINEYS REMAINED close to the O'Sullivans, Donie and Áine, all their life and great friends. A special kind of people, with an instant ability to empathise with people and draw them into a friendly circle.

The discussions in their house, particularly around sport but also delving deeply into religion, politics, current affairs… almost anything, really, were engrossing. It was there that Donie developed his close friendships with the likes of Eamonn Young and Nicky Rackard, friendships that would deepen throughout lifetimes.

One particular memory of the start of a close friendship stands out.

Mickey Ned O'Sullivan was Kerry's captain in 1975, but famously was knocked out during the final and it was fellow Kenmare man Pat Spillane who lifted the cup. In 2005, the club decided to have the cup presented to him by Dublin's captain on that fateful day, Seán Doherty at a special banquet in the INEC in Killarney as a fundraiser.

'I was having a bit of a run-in with cancer at the time', says Donie. 'I was receiving chemotherapy in the cancer unit in Tralee, and radiotherapy at Cork University Hospital. I was getting better and had just started driving again, as much to kill the monotony as anything else, when I got the invitation from Kenmare. I was humming and hawing about it.

'I didn't really want to go, but Áine persuaded me, even if it was only for a short while.'

The Dublin team had been invited, and in fairness to them, they all showed up. Dr Con Murphy from Cork, Moss Finn, and many more… Micheál Ó Muircheartaigh was the host.

'I happened to be at the same table as David Hickey and Anton O'Toole, and as you do, we fell into conversation. They obviously knew about my illness; it certainly wasn't a great secret anyway.

'When I told David that I was going to the Beaumont for treatment, he insisted on giving me his number to ring him – working there himself, he knew a lot of my medical team. I took him up on it and we have been good friends ever since.

'A great footballer, a great doctor… and an even greater human being.

'I was going to leave early… I had to, I didn't have the strength at the time for a full night out, but I didn't want to make a show of myself by leaving in front of everybody. Anton told me not to worry, he would head out to the toilet and I would follow him out.

'A simple gesture, but a very kind and thoughtful one; it tells you the measure of that man too… a man who died before his time, sadly.'

Donie and friends (from left) Brian O'Brien, Johnny Culloty, Mick O'Connell, Ned Fitzgerald and Mick Moynihan. And Donie (right) receives an award from Kerry legend Paddy Kennedy.

« EPILOGUE »

The world does not keep running because it is a paying proposition: God doesn't make a cent on the deal. The world goes on because a few good people in every generation believe in it and underwrite it with their lives. We are not kept alive by legislators, capitalists and militarists. We are kept alive by people of faith, people of vision. We need them in every generation.

— Arthur Miller (*Spirituality*)

THERE'S SOMETHING INTRINSICALLY Irish about Donie Ó Súilleabháin. Above all he is a family man – sadly, Áine's health declined and she passed away in April 2021. It was a hard and sad time for Donie, and again, his many, many friends rallied round.

His beloved Áine was gone.

'I miss her presence continually.

'We met in Dublin… a chance meeting in a million.

'She was studying medicine in UCD. We were first introduced by a friend of Áine's… it was 1965, and Áine still had a long way to go in her studies. And me?

I was quiet, and not very self-confident… a chance in a million that we would have a life together. But our brief, chance encounter became something precious.

'I went to America for a year, to study in St John's University, and our relationship lasted through that period. Áine also went to America, to Virginia a couple of years later… and we survived that too.

'We wrote to each other… for those years.

'We were married in June of 1971. Kerry had played Mayo in the National League final the previous Sunday… and Áine would have liked to see Mayo winning, as she was born there, but she wasn't that interested in football, really.

'We survived my footballing days, too.'

◄◄◆►►

COLM Ó SÚILLEABHÁIN

MY MOTHER AND father have lived in Tralee since around the time I was born, but dad would still consider Killarney his home.

When we were young, we used to go visit my grandparents in Killarney twice every week. My mother would stay in the house chatting with my grandmother, and my father would disappear for the afternoon to visit his many acquaintances in Killarney. He loves the company of the people from the Spa area… the people he grew up with and the people he played football with.

I know from talking to dad how the 1966 O'Donoghue Cup impacted on the lives of the people in Spa, and how this made a huge impression on him. That football could make these people, whom he had grown up with, proud of who they were and where they came from stayed with him. I know dad considered it a privilege that he had contributed to that. That in a way epitomises dad's attitude to his football career with county and club. He thinks that it was a great gift to have the talent and the luck to play a game he loved for so many years when he was in the prime of his life. He also feels that anything he did for Kerry and for Spa was paid back many times over.

Dad is a fierce competitor in all aspects of life, and I have no doubt it was the same when he was playing football, but I think that he values the friends he made playing more than any medals that he won. I have often seen this first hand in the last 15 years when I travelled with him to south Kerry to visit Mick O'Connell and Ned Fitzgerald.

When he speaks of people he played with and against, he is much more likely to talk about their life outside football. The one time he will mention football prowess is for former players from less successful counties who may be less well known.

When he speaks of his time playing Railway Cup he will often mention a former player from Clare, Waterford, Limerick or Tipperary and simply say, 'He was a right good player'. This is one of the highest compliments dad would give to anyone as a footballer. It was his way of acknowledging that success in football was a result of circumstance and geography as well as talent.

In a similar vein I remember a conversation between him and Mick O'Connell, where they pondered how much they would have won, and how well they might have been know, if they had born in another county.

My mother and father were married for just less than 50 years. They were in many ways quite different personalities. Mom was a quieter, gentler person than dad. She was immensely practical, busy, and hated waste, but she always had time for a cup of tea and a chat. Her family was at the centre of her life, and we all adored her.

She had very little interest in football and dad was happy enough with that. Usually, the most she would say on the subject was, 'Poor Mayo'.

Mom had dementia for the last six years of her life and dad was her primary carer. In what were often difficult times, both emotionally and physically, he never once complained and he always showed a brave face for us. These years highlighted many of the character traits I admire most about him... his energy, his fierce determination, his optimism and, most of all, his humanity and kindness.

Mom was buried in Aghadoe graveyard in Killarney, and on the day of her funeral Dr Crokes and Spa provided a guard of honour. It with a lovely and fitting tribute to both my mother and father.

In 1984 and '86, the family went to San Diego in California on two house-swap holidays while my father was working in the University of San Diego for the summer. These were two great adventures. It was a very exotic holiday for '80s Ireland'.

My father played football when he was over there with the club in San Diego, even though he was well into his forties (he had always stayed in good physical condition). These are the only memories I have of my father playing football. His kicking off the ground stands out.

He was still able to put the ball well past midfield from the kickout. I was always aware that he was known for place-kicking, so it was nice to see it in a real game.

Dad has a deep love for the Irish language.

When I visit him in Tralee, many of his conversations on the phone are 'as gaeilge' with friends like Seamus MacGearailt, Mick O'Connell, Mick Gleeson, Larry Ó Cinnéide and Micheál Ó Sé. All his children went to primary school in Scoil Mhic Easmainn in Tralee and this interest has passed onto to the next generation.

I think that attending Maynooth was very important to my father. He often speaks fondly of his time there. My uncle has told me that he had hugely improved as a footballer by the time he came back from Maynooth after his first year.

Dad often said that the inter-class matches in Maynooth were of a very high standard and that it was the making of him as a footballer. But more important than the football, my father made lifelong friends in Maynooth.

I also think that Maynooth was the place that started what became a lifelong interest in literature and history. An interest that he has imparted to me and Eoin.

FIONNUALA Ó SÚILLEABHÁIN

GROWING UP IN Kerry, I was more or less oblivious to dad's renowned skill and notoriety on the football field. It was not something he talked about a lot and I never played GAA. It was a different time, but now my own daughters have played GAA since they were very young and continue to love the game as teenagers. My four sons also love sitting with their granddad Donie and hearing his stories, examining his medals... they are very proud of what he achieved.

All of them, at one time or another, have expressed their desire to mimic their 'Donie' and become county footballers or hurlers.

We all attended Scoil Mhic Easmainn as children and all of us to this day have inherited dad's love of the Irish language. Indeed, all his grandchildren are attending or have attended a gaelscoil. Irish language has always been an integral part of our family and although my mother had roots in Connemara, it was dad who passed this love on and encouraged this in all his children. All dad's grandchildren have Irish names... Saoirse, Caoilinn, Siúin, Oran, Lochlann, Cuán, Ruairí, Cian, Síofra, Ferdia, Ailbhe and Croíadh.

My late mother was a highly intelligent, gentle and extremely patient woman, and she supported us both emotionally and academically. I was very fortunate and blessed to have had my mother as my best friend for my adult life.

She offered all her children her guidance, love, patience and wisdom. She taught me everything I know about raising children and she had such a special relationship with all my children. She supported dad with all his interests and he valued her opinion more than any other.

Dad was a formidable figure growing up… he was very committed to us achieving our potential academically and securing a fulfilling future for ourselves. His expectations were high, but we never felt they were unreasonable, as his mantra was always… 'achieve your capabilities'.

Dad was someone you discussed career decisions and financial decisions with. He wasn't a man back then for the emotional heart-warming chats… that was left to mom. She was the glue that bound us all to together. Dad was a tough, but fair parent. He grew up in relative poverty and he climbed out of it, and he wanted to make sure that all his children were protected and secure. He always wanted us to have options and, therefore, he wanted to ensure that we all received very good education and was so supportive and encouraging of this.

Dad has let us see a very different side to him in the last six to seven years as mom became sick and eventually died in April 2021. Throughout mom's illness, his strength, his stoicism and his optimism never wavered. We had a very difficult few years as a family but dad changed and adapted incredibly to embrace our difficult circumstances.

He talked to us and listened to us as we all grappled to come to terms with our beloved mother's cruel illness.

As mom declined and her communication skills rapidly deteriorated, dad took on her role. He became our friend and to this day my siblings and I speak with dad every day. We are all married with young children and dad is a huge part of all our lives. He regularly visits us in our respective homes and we all spend a lot of time in Killarney with him. Mom's illnesses let dad's softer and more emotional side shine through.

He strength and fortitude were incredible during mom's illness and my relationship with him changed significantly. Before mom's illness, my relationship with dad was one of huge respect, love and admirations. Whilst retaining all of these, my emotional connection with dad is extremely strong.

We regularly talk and reminisce about mom and how much we miss her. The void from mom's illness and subsequent death in our lives is huge and can never be filled, but dad has done an incredible job of easing this pain.

We were blessed to have had such a wonderful mother and continue to be blessed having dad in our lives.

EOIN Ó SÚILLEABHÁIN

IT WAS MANY years after the lymphoma, and its attritional treatment, before I had developed the rudimentary level of emotional intelligence to conceive of its effects on my parents... becoming a parent completed that evolution for me.

Malady and misfortune afflict all families, and I can only speak of ours. How fortunate were we to reach the far shore without a scratch on the hull. At least, how fortunate was I, that such a danger should strike at too young an age to contemplate mortality.

The mental torment my parents must have endured (Colm and Fionnuala too) are not to be envied.

Throughout the months of obligatory isolation (due to the weakening of my immune system and susceptibility to infection), dad arranged visits from names in football that dazzled my mind's pantheon. Paradoxically, two of my best memories are actually related to hurling; it may have seemed a bit more exotic at that age.

On one of the many hot summer days of 1989, Johnny Culloty paid a visit and pucked around with me in the back garden for what seemed like hours. To have a man who played Railway Cup deign to do so was some privilege. The second event was when Eddie Murphy, the Kerry hurler, called, and left me a sliotar used in a recent match when they shocked Clare.

This I used to bring with me to Crumlin as a talisman. It would take me a while to track it down right now, but I know exactly where his wing forward's jersey from the day is kept.

What has been said about his living through my illness, and about his lingering relationships after his career finished, manifests most patently whenever I hear of a former teammate or rival who has been diagnosed with a grave medical condition or who has suffered bereavement.

Although they may not have been in any frequent contact for years, dad will make a visit a priority, and it will not be a solo call. 'This seeing the sick endears them to us, us too it endears', from Felix Randal *by Gerard Manley Hopkins is one of his most cherished quotations. His patience and kindness when nursing mom during her final illness, of course, was the toughest of all.*

The readiness to cite the likes of Hopkins is another reason to be grateful to dad. He fostered a love of learning in us; foremost in the various fields comes literature, with history and politics featuring highly. We have been bestowed a constant thirst for knowledge (whether practical or not is a different matter).

His sentiments on the development of Cumann Lúthchleas Gael would tie into his most fundamental values – integrity, altruism and a profound aversion to narcissism. He taught us neither to haughtily cast aside the old, nor mindlessly embrace the new, without first investing some independent thought in the matter.

For three decades dad has spoken often about the 1990 NFL final.

Who played, who won… if the game was abandoned, these are irrelevant, only that I was there alongside him, with Colm. For many years I would be bashful at this focus on me, and often wished the subject to be diverted to another sibling's prowesses or problems.

My self-consciousness, however, has long since given way to pride in dad's sense of perspective.

Not that he does not care deeply about football, but that he sees its primary value as a social medium, a needle that can knit communities together, rather than as a medal or score count. The friendships that he has made through football have outlived any gaisce on the field.

And if this is not what Cumann Lúthchleas Gael should be about, then there is little left to play for.

ORNA Ó SÚILLEABHÁIN

DAD NEVER PUT pressure on us to follow in his footsteps when it came to sport.

He was far more concerned that we fulfil our academic rather than sporting potential. Lucky for me, given that the peak of my sporting career was getting to the semi-final of the Tralee mini-Sevens football competition with the Sixth Class girls from Scoil Mhic Easmainn. Dad was there to support on that day… I think his favourite moment was when I kicked a point instead of taking an open goal opportunity!

Mom wasn't much of a sports enthusiast, but held out hope that her native Mayo would one day win back the Sam Maguire Cup, having memories of their wins in the 1950s.

My parents married on a Tuesday in June 1971, two days after dad had captained Kerry to beat Mayo in the league final. They were married for almost 50 years and she was a wonderful mother and an incredibly supportive wife, never holding dad back from his sports or his travels.

He in turn supported her fiercely through her illness in recent years, never complaining during what were very challenging times for all of us, but most of all for him. We miss her every day.

◄◄◆▷►

AT HIS CORE, Donie is a small farmer's son from a rural community outside Killarney, and the simple values inculcated in him from the very beginning are still at the core of the man. He carried them with him as his horizons expanded all over the world.

He loved those experiences and was able to fit in anywhere.

He has a special affinity for San Diego (where the popular lecturer in Irish Studies has been Grand Marshal of the St Patrick's Day parade) and New York. In both cities, he is at 'home' – and in San Diego, memorably, the O'Sullivan family summered twice.

In 1984, in Donie's first summer at the University of San Diego – just like in New York and San Francisco – he and his family felt the warm embrace of the GAA community six thousand miles from 'home'. And Donie found the friendship of Mick Ward, Peter Smith, Timmy O'Donovan, Jim Foley, Tony McDonnell and Mick Byrne, amongst many other great GAA men.

Donie, *A Footballer Once…* well, he had moved onto a different chapter in his life.

San Diego was central to that life. Though, in January 2005, when Donie had his 'brush', as he describes it, with cancer, there was no travelling… anywhere.

'We were heading to the west coast, but the doctor rang me the night before and he wanted me in the next day to do a biopsy… a needle biopsy.'

Donie was eventually diagnosed with Hodgkin's Lymphoma. His treatment included chemotherapy and radiotherapy in Cork.

'The radiotherapy treatment in Cork was easy compared to the chemotherapy protocol before that. I met up with so many friends from my football days. We had cups of tea, or lunch…'

Donie Ó Súilleabháin is not a complainer or dramatist.

◄ ◄ ◆ ► ►

EOIN Ó SÚILLEABHÁIN

In October of 2022, Colm and myself joined dad for his latest Californian holiday. There were to be two main bases of operation– San Diego and San Francisco, naturally enough.

Having negotiated the ulcer-inducing traffic of Los Angeles, we decamped on the tied island of Coronado, effectively an exclave of San Diego, connected only by a tombolo in the style of Howth Head. Here we stayed with a friend of dad's named Peadar MacGabhann (or colloquially, Pete Smith). They first encountered one another a half century ago up in San Francisco, when Pete, originally an Abbeylara native, was still based in Alaska. Married to a Mexican lady, Elluie, we were indulged in all the comfort and indulgence possible, and asked for nothing.

We were blessed with good fortune, as an old family friend was working in Los Angeles, and braved the lethal freeway in order to bring us out to dinner. Kevin Cronin had been (along with the rest of his family) a neighbour in Tralee and a friend in Boston after he emigrated nearly four decades ago. His mother had babysat us; his father was a distant cousin of dad's.

Our northward journey we spread over two days. Bypassing that aforementioned sprawling metropolis, we returned to the Pacific coast at Ventura; hugging the ocean as far as Santa Barbara, we diverted inland to savour the spectacle of the San Rafael and Santa Ynez ranges, before passing through the uniquely Danish village of Solvang, then westering again to enjoy the sun 'declining beneath the blue sea'.

After bivouacking in the town of San Luis Obispo, we drove on through Big Sur of renown, hemmed in between the precipices of the Santa Lucia mountains and the boundless waters. An obligatory burger in Monterey fuelled us for the home straight, before the ubiquitous fog of that fabled bay enveloped us. We had travelled the mundane inland route in 1984 over one gruelling day; I shall leave it to the reader to guess which was more enjoyable.

Here we were privileged to experience the marvellous hospitality of dad's fellow Spa man, Denis Casey, and his wife Victoria. Although the cloud never dispersed, it dented neither our enjoyment of Angel Island, nor our drive north to the wine country around Petaluma. On our last night, we finally persuaded our hosts to be treated to dinner, before climbing on board the inevitable cable car home.

For me, the two houses perfectly encapsulated either end of the spectrum of our father's friends. The first, a man who has spent easily the majority of his life as an exile; such is the usual nature of friendship with dad, that 15 years later he had a ready contact and guide to San Diego, when we shared his first summer there. The second, a man of the next generation in a city infrequently visited by dad, where the ties of townland, parish and community remain unfrayed.

However, the unexpected highlight of our holiday (and I think the other two would concur) was our sojourn to an unremarkable blue collar town called El Cajón, about 30 kilometres east of San Diego. Here we drove into an anonymous corner of the suburbs, up to the end of a cul de sac with the misleadingly romantic name of Starview Drive.

The lure of this bait was impalpable to anybody else, but here we had stayed on our house share for six weeks in 1984. The memories were many and recalled with ease, although now accompanied with a bittersweet lining, having lost mom within what still seems so recent a time.

There was little to do but loiter and take a few photographs, spending 10 minutes for the sake of an hour's drive, but there was an unspoken bond and serenity on that return journey that shall be cherished as long as one of us remains in this realm.

◄ ◄ ◆ ► ►

LIFE ALWAYS CONTAINS twists and turns. Sometimes it contains a precipice, and that's how it felt for Donie and Áine in May of 1989.

'Eoin was just 10 years old at the time and he had a clinging cold that wouldn't go away. We didn't pay too much attention to it, to be honest, but it wasn't clearing up, so Áine told me that she would take him down to the hospital to get it looked at.'

This isn't an easy story for Donie to tell.

His love for his children pours from the man; his eldest Colm, then Fionnuala, Eoin and finally Orna. And his love for his 12 grandchildren pours afresh.

Of course, the dawning horror of Eoin's illness, and brush with death that was far too close, is as fresh in his mind now as it was then. 'She took him in and rang me straightaway; they knew it was serious. They told me that Eoin was seriously ill. Paediatrician and x-ray radiologist Hilary Kelly from Down quickly diagnosed aggressive lymphoma... the hospital were brilliant, I'd say Áine being their colleague helped.

'They told her that we had to go to Crumlin immediately.

'They didn't know what type of lymphoma it was, but it was cancerous, it was progressive, and life-threatening. I got there as fast as I could and we set out straightaway. We didn't tell the neighbours the details, didn't contact the kids... nothing. Thankfully, our neighbours were very good.

'It was the longest drive of my life. I can still remember every twist and turn of the road. The weather was beautiful, but Eoin was getting progressively worse.

'We arrived at Crumlin Children's Hospital... Dr Finn Breatnach was the paediatric oncologist. We were just sitting there in a state of shock, really; this was the last thing anyone could have expected.

'Dr Breatnach drained fluid from his lungs later that night.'

Eoin was officially diagnosed the following day and Dr Breatnach established treatment protocols. 'He was there for a long time. Myself and Áine took turns travelling up and down to be with him. It was a very scary time for all of us. Orna was in hospital as well, in Tralee, suffering with asthma.

'We were dreading the phone ringing with bad news.'

Finally came some encouraging news.

DONIE WENT UP to Dublin on the morning train (Áine had come down the night before) and headed straight into the hospital. It was four days after Eoin's admittance, and Orna was out of hospital.

'On the way in, Dr Breatnach came over to me with a beaming smile. "Did you see the x-rays?"

'His excitement made it seem like it was going to be good news, but you're almost scared to hope at that stage. He actually ran and got the x-rays and showed them to me, saying, "Isn't it great?".

'Now, I had no clue about how to read an x-ray... how could I? And he realised that and told me, "It's working!"

'Lifting Sam Maguire, as wonderful as that was, couldn't remotely compare to that feeling.

'There were other children in the cancer ward – Eoin was amazed and a bit frightened that a lot of the other children were bald from the treatment. He was told that it would have to happen to him as well, but that he would be able to have a wig if he wanted. Some news for a 10-year-old child to hear!

'Looking back, you'd go in feeling sorry for yourself, thinking you are the only one in that situation. Then you realise that there are people who have it much worse. When you get past it, there's a feeling of guilt. You can't help thinking of all those children who never make it home.

'He was there for a couple of weeks. Once Dr Breatnach deemed him to be getting a bit of strength back, he wanted him to go home – the psychological effects of that would be important along with his treatment. He was still very weak, though.

'I went back to work. In hindsight, of course, I shouldn't have.

'I had agreed to supervise the Leaving Cert Exams in Causeway Comprehensive. Eoin had a kind of tube that we had to put into his main vein to administer his medicine; it had to be washed three or four times a day. Áine turned around to check on Eoin – and he suddenly convulsed and lost consciousness. Luckily, Colm was home for lunch, he was doing his own Leaving at the time.

'He brought Eoin out to the car, while Áine made a crash call to the hospital, and she rushed him in. They put him on life support straightaway. It was June 7, 1989.

'I was in Causeway, not knowing any of this. Until there was a knock on the door and I looked over to see Seán Óg Sheehy and Fr Liam Comer. I knew instantly that something awful had happened.

'Poor Colm had to go back and do English Paper 2 in the evening, not knowing whether his brother was alive. Áine and myself came home from the hospital around 7pm. Neighbours were calling…

'Eoin hung on during the day, and continued in a coma throughout. Dermot Spillane, the surgeon, stayed with us all night in that little room. Marie Whelan, the sister in charge, was just terrific in every way.

'Eoin appeared to have no chance of surviving, and we were thinking and then discussing when the life support would be unplugged. He had been anointed earlier. I called the family at home to come in. That was a sober gathering, to say the least. One by one, Eoin's brother and sisters were going in to Eoin to say goodbye to him.'

'Then, many hours later, Eoin squeezed Fionnuala's hand.

'Ah, I thought that it was a hope-induced hallucination in the poor child. But it happened again. He came round very slowly on the Thursday morning. We took Colm in to him, and Colm told me that he couldn't talk but that he had asked him to write a bit.

'When he was able to go home at last, we were told that it would be a long convalescence. It was very hard for Eoin to keep his spirits up. I brought him to Tiernaboul a few times a week, wearing his wig. He was very self-conscious about it, the same as anybody would be at that age. He told me that if the hair went again, he wouldn't be fighting on anymore.

'I hardly knew what to say to him.

'People are very good, though. Without the goodness of humanity, I doubt if we would have survived it all. All of the medical staff we encountered, every last one of them, went far above and beyond their jobs to help us and Eoin in every possible way they could. We will never be able to say enough about Finn Breatnach... an incredible man.

'Our neighbours couldn't have given us any more support than they did. The whole community. Just everyone, and we needed all of it.'

It took a long time, but Eoin Ó Súilleabháin made a full recovery.

DANIEL PATRICK O'SULLIVAN, of course, was more than *A Footballer, Once.*

He is a former Kerry football captain.

One of a select group of Kerrymen who had the great honour of lifting the Sam Maguire Cup on behalf of his club and county.

Donie has almost forgotten one story.

A story about that captaincy, and a letter he received the week of the All-Ireland final. And a photograph of Donie, minutes before the game commenced, going down on one knee and kissing the ring of the Archbishop of Cashel, as patron of the GAA.

Except there would be no such photograph!

For decade after decade, captains of All-Ireland football and hurling teams in Croke Park kissed the Bishop's ring in front of the throngs of supporters. Donie and Meath captain, Jack Quinn, would have done the same before the 1970 All-Ireland final.

'I received a typed letter... from a Redemptorist priest,' explains Donie. 'Jack Quinn, I was informed was receiving the same letter, as was the referee Paul Kelly.

'It was a very nice letter, well written and to the point.

'The priest wrote that the custom of kissing the ring went back to feudal times, and he asked me to not do it… not to bend my knee and kiss the ring.

'He explained that it was not a spiritual gesture, that it was a gesture from medieval times… a symbol of temporal power.'

Donie spoke to nobody in the county board. He made up his own mind.

As the minutes counted down, and the Archbishop of Cashel was introduced to the rival captains, Donie shook his hand.

As did Jack Quinn. And the match referee.

'I'd say Archbishop Morris, a humble man, was quite relieved we weren't making a spectacle in front of him!' Donie now reflects. There would be no more kissing in Croke Park from September of 1970 on.

DONIE ENJOYS POETRY.

And most poets.

Sigerson Clifford is one such poet, born in 1913 and reared in Cahersiveen. One of his works, titled *Kerry's Footballers* comes from his collection *Ballads of a Bogman*.

Donie admires the anonymity shown in the poem to every Kerry footballer who ever lived. Not one great footballer is mentioned.

Neither does the Kerry team in the poem belong to any one man. Donie Ó Súilleabháin takes delight noting that not one Kerry football team ever was in the personal possession, or forever more should be thought of as ever being the property, of a man lucky enough to be honoured with the task of training or managing a successful team from the county.

Sigerson Clifford writes the words… *Our Kerry*.

Donie loves that…

Green and gold, and lithe limbs leaping when our Kerry played Kildare.

The Kerry football team always has, and always will, belong to its people.

KERRY'S FOOTBALLERS
BY SIGERSON CLIFFORD

Plough or spade or seinboat shaped them for the deeds they were to do,
Street and school and mountain heard their victory cry,
Now their memories arch like rainbows o'er the meadows of the mind,
The Alive who'll live forever, and the Dead who'll never die.

When the stranger came steel-fisted and the hounds bayed in the glen,
O, my Kingdom of the half-doors and the white wet window sills,
Where the gun-smoke wrote its message there the great footballing men
Fought the flame-red rearguard battle of the hills.

O, the gold bells of the old days tinkle wistful in my mind
And I see the fireman dark against the light,
Hear the whistle whimper lonely o'er the dead leaves of the years
As the ghost train races swiftly through the night.

These the men your fathers spoke of in the game your fathers loved,
These the men who blazed the trail and made it fair.
In my dreaming now I see them as I saw them long ago,
Green and gold, and lithe limbs leaping when our Kerry played Kildare.

Donie and Áine, and also their family (Fionnuala, Colm, Eoin and Orna). Colm, Donie and Eoin together in Croke Park in 1990, as they celebrate a 'battle' won.

Made in United States
North Haven, CT
11 March 2023

33930234R00125